BONDS OF IRON

JAMES OSTERHAUS, Ph.D.

GARY J. OLIVER, Ph.D.,
GENERAL EDITOR

MOODY PRESS
CHICAGO

© 1994 by
JAMES OSTERHAUS

All Scripture quotations, unless indicated, are taken from the *Holy Bible, New International Version®*. NIV®. Copyright © 1973, 1978, 1984 International Bible Society. Used by permission of Zondervan Publishing House. All rights reserved.

ISBN 0-8024-7129-3

1 3 5 7 9 10 8 6 4 2

Printed in the United States of America

To Dad, Maj, Butch, and Win—
four men who helped mold me,
and then became my friends

CONTENTS

FOREWORD

The facts are clear: millions of men are friendless. Many of these men are highly successful in their careers, leaders in their communities and churches, well respected, and even admired. But the fact remains that there is no other man with whom they feel comfortable to share their fears and weaknesses, hopes and dreams, triumphs and failures.

It has not always been this way. Over the course of history, many men have invested themselves in male friends. The biblical record tells of the deep, sacrificial friendship of David and Jonathan. St. Augustine called friendship the highest form of love. In our day, members of a fresh breed of men are committing themselves to each other in a significant way. In this book you will meet two of them involved in a strong, close relationship—Richard Halverson and Doug Coe (Chapter 7)—and several others, including Jerry White and Fred Hignell III.

Richard and Doug and Jerry and Fred are among a growing number of men who recognize the need to develop intentional relationships with other men—relationships that go beyond common interests and hobbies, shop talk, and Monday Night Football. They have made friendships a priority. They understand that God made us for friendship and that the American ideal of the rugged individualist standing invulnerable to the world often cloaks a man's deep insecurity, an inability to trust, and a real longing for relationship.

Reinforced with rich stories of men who have experienced the reality of God-centered relationships, *Bonds of Iron* contains sage and practical counsel.

Such counsel can come only from one who has lived what he writes. Jim Osterhaus is a man whose life has been deeply affected by his relationships with other men. I have observed firsthand the influence he has had as a friend and mentor to my own son, Kevin. And Jim has thought carefully and deeply about what goes into making life-changing friendships.

If you will read, heed, and put Jim's good counsel into practice, you may well find that your own life with God as well as your interactions with others will be deeper and richer.

LEIGHTON FORD

ACKNOWLEDGMENTS

I need not acknowledge all the friends who have been my guiding inspiration as I was formulating this book, for you will be meeting them in the following pages. I would, however, like to mention several people whose input was instrumental in developing the material in its present form.

First, I thank my wife, Marcy, who has tolerated me, given me feedback, and generally been my best friend—not only throughout this project but during almost twenty-five years of marriage. Without her constant companionship, I doubt I'd accomplish much of anything in my life.

I am also grateful to Dr. Gary Oliver for his support and assistance in this project. He is becoming a dear friend, and I cherish the times he and I can spend together.

Finally, I'm very grateful to Doug Coe and Dick Halverson for allowing me to invade their personal lives to talk about their very special friendship (see chapter 7). Their friendship is unique, and their willingness to share it with a wide audience has been very gratifying to me.

Introduction

PERSONAL STORIES

Beyond the information and recommendations, this is a book of stories. You'll find my own personal story here, as well as those of Butch, Win, Doug, Ed, Jim, Joe, Rich, Steve, Tom, Bill, Roger, John, Kevin, Dan, Ron, Gordon, and Gary. You'll also meet Martyn, Jerry, Peter, Wendall, Charlie, Glenn, Kelly, and many other men whom I've had the privilege of having as friends over the years. In many ways, my life can be measured by the presence of particular friends through the years.

The family in which I grew up emphasized the value of friendships. My mother constantly stressed to my sister, brother, and me the importance of seeking, nurturing, and maintaining friendships. My mother and father both then modeled friendship to us by seeking and enjoying numerous friends. As a result, the three of us can point to many friends who have been pivotal in our lives over the years.

You'll also find the stories of other men, maybe some that you've heard of, men who have experienced friendship from many different angles. As much as anything, friendship is about personal stories, the unfolding stories of relationships that reach back through time.

I've tried to look at these stories, think about them, and distill from them the essence of what friendship is all about. That's been a formidable task, for friendships are complex. But I think I've been able to see trends here, and from the trends develop principles. I've also borrowed from the thinking of others. Many people in the past have thought long on friendship. In fact, the ancients cherished friendship more deeply than we do. They also nourished the tender sprouts of friendship in ways that we now find unfamiliar. St. Augustine, in *The City of God*, described friendship as the highest form of human love. He explained that he prayed for friendship and sought to develop it with all of his energy.

The word for friend that has been handed down to us through the centuries comes from the Saxon word *freond*, which means one who is beloved or free. This certainly gives us a glimpse into the thinking of people long ago who thought of this unique relationship. And the elements of a friend remain the same today: The friend is one who is loved, who is bound by the commitments that love implies. But the friend is also free, free to become all he was created to be. As this book unfolds, we will see how accurate these definitions are, for, indeed, friendship means being loved and being free.

In some ways we men just don't know how to talk about relationships. We grope around, looking for words, but we seem to have a terrible time describing what friendship is all about and how to develop a friendship. We mix up our concepts as we mix up our words. In speaking of a friend, we don't know how to describe our feelings.

"Love sounds too strong," men have told me. "How can I say 'I love Bob'? Love is for wife and family. He's a guy. I guess I'll say that he's a good bud." With mixed words and mixed concepts, it becomes increasingly difficult for us to identify the particulars of any relationship.

As we explore the paths of friendship in this book, we will be able to at least begin to flesh out some of these concepts and understand them more easily.

Within the past couple of years, men have begun to take a more penetrating look at themselves to see what makes them 'tick.' Issues once considered off limits now are open for discussion, as more men are willing to be honest and vulnerable. Men are more willing to consider and express their emotions, as pointed out in Gary Oliver's *Real Men Have Feelings Too*, the first book in the Men of Integrity series. Yet men still face a cultural stigma in that they are not really allowed to mention their wounds, let alone discuss them at length. Men have to "be strong," "buck up," "play hurt." Well, we have played hurt, and we've paid for it too.

For many of us, there's been a revival in interest among men about just being together, being together in ways that have felt foreign to many of us. As we've learned about ourselves and felt more comfortable expressing to other men what we've experienced, we've naturally begun to build friendships.

I trust this book will help men who are either in the process of building friendships or who are now at least considering the place of friendship in their lives. As you read these stories—all true—remember that behind each story is an important truth. (Some names in the stories have been changed for reasons of privacy.)

At the end of each chapter are instructions for projects and short responses in the "Take Action" section; in the text itself, some chapters also ask you to do things. Take some time to do each one. Probably the best way to go through this book is with a friend, or in a small group of men. Thinking through the concepts and discussing each in the company of others would be an excellent way to apply the ideas in this book. Also consider writing your thoughts and impressions in a journal as you read and discuss the book. This could be kept as a few sheets of paper in the back of your appointment book. Use the journal to set goals for yourself regarding friendships. You may also use the journal to record the answers to questions and exercises that you will find at various places in the book.

How can we as men develop and maintain genuine friendhips? This book tries to answer that question. When we answer the question—when we forge lasting relationships—bonds of iron join and make us strong and whole.

Let's begin by considering why men often fear the very thing they need—good, caring friends.

1

DO YOU FEAR FRIENDSHIPS?

There was his name, neatly scripted in the inside cover of the book. I stared in disbelief. "John Nelson." I had retrieved the book from a box of books that were being donated to a church library. The title had intrigued me: *The Art of Friendship.* But when I saw to whom the book had once belonged, I was shocked.

John Nelson had been a shy man. Not really withdrawn, but quiet and polite. He would carry on normal conversations and looked pretty much like everyone else. He'd even become involved in things around the church, volunteering his talents from time to time. He was married and had several kids. John and his wife had been members of a small group within the church. He held a respectable job. I don't think that anyone had quite figured out why John had driven off that clear, crisp winter day, found a quiet place far from everyone, and put a bullet through his head.

And now here I stood, holding his book on building friendships. I wondered if he had ever had friendships. If so, why had those friendships failed when he needed them the most?

In stark contrast to John's tragic life is the friendship between Jerry White, international president of The Navigators, and Fred Hignell III, a real estate developer. These two men, admit-

tedly unlikely candidates to be friends, met over ten years ago;
they detailed their friendship in two recent magazine articles.[1]
They began to pray for each other and hold each other accountable. "We both are probing the spiritual and personal areas of our
lives" and asking for counsel when tough decisions arise, Jerry
explained.

Then tragedy struck the White family. Jerry's adult son was
found murdered while Jerry and his wife, Mary, were off speaking
at a conference. Once notified, the couple jumped in their car and
sped home to find Fred already there, waiting for them. Through
the difficult days ahead, Fred was at his friend's side.

Jerry explained those difficult days this way: "Most of my life
I had been the strong one, self-sufficient, helping others through
hard times. Now I really needed others. I was weak and unsure
where my emotions would be from day to day—guilt, sorrow,
fear, or just weariness. Fred sensed my mood and shared Scripture or just prayed."[2] Even after the initial days of trauma were
finished, Fred continued to call and help his friend Jerry work
through the grief process, and hold him accountable in his heavy
work and speaking schedule to do what was needed to maintain
himself and his family spiritually, emotionally, and physically.

"Fred did a lot of listening, and at times, he gave strong
counsel," Jerry explained. "His help was indispensable as it
strengthened me to help my wife and Julie, Steve's young widow,
and our three daughters in their time of deep need. In particular,
Fred helped me through feelings of guilt that I had not spent
enough time with Steve. I felt I should have been more attentive
or traveled less in his younger years. Fred confronted me with the
fact that guilt was not justified and I needed to trust God for the
past."[3]

Jerry summed up his relationship with his friend Fred and
the crisis they weathered together this way: "Like nothing else,
this experience has shown me the value of an accountability relationship."

MADE FOR FRIENDSHIPS, YET—

We were created to be in relationship. In fact, some theolo-
gians have argued that to be made in God's image is to be in relationship—in relationship to God first, then to others. It's not an
option. It's as human as breathing. Interestingly, in Genesis 1–2,

as God is creating everything, He pronounces a benediction on each new wonder: "It was good." Also significant is what He found to be not good. He creates man and realizes it's not good that the man is alone. At this point, God creates another person to be with him, to relate to him, to drive out the aloneness.

To be truly human, exhibiting God's image, is to be in relationship with other people. . . . In spite of this, most men, including men who know Christ, put relationships on the back burner.

Why is relationship so central to the image of God in humans? It's central to our image and experience because it's central to who God is. God has relationship within His own person—within the Trinity—even without anyone else. He knows relationship because from the beginning he has experienced relationship Himself, within the three persons of the Godhead. When He created us and made us in His image, quite naturally relationship became central to that image. To be truly human, exhibiting God's image, is to be in relationship with other people.

In spite of this, most men, including men who know Christ, put relationships on the back burner. I've been a counselor for nearly twenty years, and I've watched hundreds of men respond to the presence and concerned involvement of another man. During the past generation, the counseling profession has given men in particular permission to come and talk. The results in many cases have been astounding. Men have eagerly responded, as if being presented a banquet of food after being in solitary on bread and water all of their lives. Maybe your experience as a man has been similar to the experience I have heard recited over and over, "I'm surrounded by people, and yet I'm unable to reach out in any meaningful way and form lasting, deep relationships."

For some time my friend Jim had served as a high-ranking government employee. He'd been to all the right schools and had a résumé that was enviable. Then one brisk morning he stepped out of his house and headed for the bus to ride to work. A cabbie on drugs was driving the wrong way down the road and flattened Jim as he stepped into the street. For several months he lingered between life and death in a coma. Eventually he emerged from his unconsciousness, but the slow, arduous task of recovery had just begun.

After many tough months, Jim's recovery was complete. But the tough times weren't. Within months of his recovery, Jim watched his wife, Carol, suffer through periods of dizziness. Though only in her young forties, Carol had real trouble steadying herself. After a number of tests she was diagnosed with multiple sclerosis. Thus began a slow, ten-year deterioration. Last year, Carol died, and Jim was alone.

But Jim had steadied himself prior to Carol's death and endured it well, though he did grieve for his wife. One reason he endured was a friendship. During Carol's illness, Jim was still struggling to get back on his feet occupationally and worked for a time for our church; eventually, though, he found himself unemployed. It was about this time that I decided to get together with Jim on a Tuesday morning for breakfast. He and I had known each other as fellow parishioners. Later we knew each other better when we both served on the church staff. So my suggesting the breakfast didn't come "out of the blue."

> *"Same time next week" became a refrain that both of us needed to help anchor our lives firmly in relationship.*

I don't remember much of that first breakfast. We talked about life in general, and some of Jim's struggles in particular.

"It's really been tough recently. Carol's situation is very taxing on me. And now I'm out networking, trying to find a job."

I had no answers. At the moment there were no answers. But Jim was hurting and needed a friend. We agreed to get together the next Tuesday at the same time in the same restaurant. Thus began a three-year ritual of getting together each Tuesday morning for breakfast.

I think at first I did it to help out a man I knew was struggling with life. But as time passed, I looked forward to our times together as much as Jim did. "Same time next week" became a refrain that both of us needed to help anchor our lives firmly in relationship. It isn't that we discussed earth-shaking problems each week. Quite the contrary, we were just there with each other. Oh, yes, the struggles did come and go. Jim's wife would have the medical crises. He found a new job and made the transition into it. I had to make one of the pivotal decisions of my vocational life. But these issues were sprinkled among the mundane occurrences of life. That's the way life is: Millions of seemingly superfluous events punctuated occasionally by that earth-shattering moment in time.

This three-year weekly ritual came to a halt when I came to Jim with my ultimate challenge. "Jim, I've been asked by a church in California to come and direct a counseling center for them. What do you think?" My friend Jim was stunned, as were all my other friends who had known me for years.

"Well, this comes as a shock," Jim was finally able to respond after he had caught his breath. "Let's go through all of the pros and cons and see if it makes any sense for you to consider moving out there." Over the next weeks we wrestled with the decision together. I decided to move my family three thousand miles away and assume this new position.

The friendship was in place to steady me when the big decision came up. Interestingly, if we have not cultivated friendships during the routine, uneventful days of our lives, when the crises do come (and they will come, for all of us), we can't run out and strike up the deep, sustaining friendship on the spur of the moment.

Bill was in such a fix. He came into my office and slumped in his chair, barely making eye contact. His marriage of twenty-three years was shaky and seemed to be unraveling. In his slow, methodical way, Bill detailed his life. "I go to work at 6, return home for a bite to eat around 6 at night. Then I go downstairs to work on my computer. Weekends were spent puttering around the house. The cast of characters in my life was dreadfully small." Basically he had centered his whole life on his family (though he chose to ignore them most of the time). There were no real friends in his life.

And now a crisis was unfolding in Bill's life. After I had only seen Bill for three sessions, his wife announced that she was leaving. She promptly packed her bags and exited. Bill was totally thrown into confusion. All the props that had held him in place were kicked out. He was alone, and he knew it.

"How about friends?" I asked as Bill nervously fingered his coffee cup and slouched in his chair in my office.

"Friends? Well, I really haven't anyone that I could call a friend. I've got a couple of guys at the office. We talk every now and then. But that's about it."

Bill was facing the most stressful time of his life. I knew he'd be in the middle of a maelstrom for months to come as this whole situation played itself. And in the midst of the crisis, Bill had no one to be with.

As the weeks passed, I realized that Bill cherished his times each week when he came to see me. He'd never had a relationship with another man like this before. Using our relationship in counseling, I was able to guide Bill toward other friendships, and he now enjoys a small group of men where he not only has companionship, but accountability.

MEN WITHOUT FRIENDS

Let's get it right out here in the open: most men just plain don't have friends. Researcher George Barna conducted extensive investigations into American lifestyles and compiled the results in *What Americans Believe*. Barna states, "Americans are among the loneliest people on earth." And how do men handle this shocking revelation? Thirty-three percent reported that they spent less time this year than last year with friends. Things aren't getting better, they're getting worse.[4]

Oh, yes, we have buddies, acquaintances, pals—people we go to the ball game with. But as educator David Smith writes, "Men find it hard to accept the fact that they need the deep fellowship with other men." They then don this mantle of, 'I'm OK alone. I don't need anyone else,' and head off into the sunset. When the yearnings for fellowship begin to awaken in us, we manufacture reasons to be together.[5]

People come to me in crisis. Few folks would ever seek out a counselor when things are going well. I've had men in my office who have lost everything—wife, children, business, fortune, good name. Man after man has faced me and had to confess, "You know, I really don't have any friends. Just a few guys at the office, or at church that I bum around with every now and then." It's at these moments of intense crisis when we begin to realize how vulnerable we really are, and how critical it is that we have friends involved in our lives.

WHY WE RESIST FRIENDS

But it doesn't take those traumatic moments in our lives to underscore the importance of friendships. Most of us know there is strength and comfort in the presence of a friend. Still, most of us seem to fear friendships, even resist them. Why? Often in friendships we fear that we will miss two elements that are crucial to healthy relationships: safety and love. So we avoid making friends altogether. Let's look at our fears and how we can have these two elements, safety and love, become part of our own friendships.

Feeling Safe

You must feel safe to relate to me. If safety isn't in place, you will feel afraid, and everything else in the relationship stops. Safety rests at the bottom of all relationships. And at the base of safety there must be a promise. Promises kept are the glue that hold together relationships. When I keep my promises, I make you feel safe because you can trust me (we'll discuss this more later).

At the core of our brains is the brain stem and limbic system, elements that evaluate a person and situation to determine just one thing, *Am I safe? Will I survive?* In his book *You've Got to Believe to be Heard,* communication expert Bert Decker explains that part of the brain doesn't use reason, doesn't think logically, the way the frontal lobes do. Here, in the "Survival Brain" (Decker also calls it the First Brain), is the seat of the emotions.[6]

Because this Survival Brain acts on emotion, and not on logic, it reacts to different signals coming from people. In each situation with every person we meet, the Survival Brain is monitoring one thing: *Is this person safe? Can I trust him?* It's as simple as that, for the Survival Brain's main concern has to do with survival.

Obviously, the question of survival precedes all other questions. If someone is going to harm you, or at least you pick up signals from the person that tell you he could possibly be a danger to you, naturally you will be wary of anything he has to say. You're going to be concerned for your own safety. The Survival Brain thus acts as a gatekeeper, determining who is safe and therefore who you will permit to speak with you and who you will ignore. "The Gatekeeper has complete power to grant or deny access to our listener's higher analytical and decision-making processes," Decker writes.[7]

As we approach people, an intuitive something way down inside tells us whether this person is safe and should be approached, or more ominous and should be approached with caution, or avoided. All of this is done quite outside of our awareness.

As small infants, as we are held and cuddled and spoken to— aunts, uncles, brothers, and sisters making all kinds of crazy faces into the crib—the information makes its way to our Survival Brains, telling us that these people (our moms to begin with) are safe people and thus can be trusted. Psychologists state that the first developmental task of all humans that must be confronted and mastered is that of trust. *Can I trust you? Are you safe?* Of course, trust and safety are closely allied; you feel safe with those you trust.

So we have all of those facial expressions, tonal sounds, and postures imprinted early in our Survival Brains, then we grow up and take all of this information with us into the world. As we approach people, there's an intuitive something way down inside that tells us whether this person is safe and should be approached, or more ominous and should be approached with caution, or avoided. All of this is done quite outside of our awareness, so we never really have a good sense as to why we're attracted to some people and repulsed by others. We just do it intuitively.

Certain people who have been badly abused in childhood generally don't trust anyone completely, because their first care-givers were themselves unsafe people. They didn't keep their promises to their children to protect them. As a result, adult men and women who were abused as children have "smoke detectors" stuck on, alerting them to danger, even when there is no fire. These people have great difficulty getting close to anyone, for they're chronically on a state of alert, and feel unsafe with everyone. If you suffered abuse as a child, your ability to trust now has been hindered.

If you find that you are having trouble with trust, here are several things you can begin doing right now. First, identify where the problem lies (people are not totally distrustful of everyone, in every area, all the time). Ask yourself two questions: What people in my life do I not feel safe with? In what situations don't I feel safe? Be as specific as you can and begin to see if a pattern emerges.

Second, draw a big circle on a piece of paper. Divide the circle into four quadrants. At the top put the word *spiritual*, at the left the word *physical*, at the right the word *social*, at the bottom *emotional*. Now think through the unsafe people you've identified, and write each name in a quadrant that is appropriate.

As an example, you might find that some females make you feel unsafe. Then you might narrow this to females who are your same age (older and younger ones don't seem to bother you). Then you might discover that women your age in social situations make you feel unsafe. So write the names of several women your age you've known in the social quadrant that have made you feel unsafe.

Third, challenge the validity of the danger. Ask yourself, *Do I really need to feel in danger with the person(s) I've identified in these situations?* To begin your challenge, think of people who are in the same categories as those who make you feel unsafe, but who do not make you feel unsafe. Why are these people an exception?

Fourth, find someone to whom you can talk about those areas where you feel unsafe. If you have a great deal of trouble in this area, you might want to find a caring Christian counselor to help.

Close friendship provides for us safe places and safe people, people that we can trust. Because close friendships are wrapped in promises that count.

Feeling Loved

The word *love* is very difficult for most men to handle. When I was preparing to move to California to direct a church counseling center, Doug, a member of that California church, contacted me by letter before I made the move. I don't think I've ever received a letter quite like it. Doug was a corporate type who had also served in the church in various voluntary capacities for some years. Years before, he had lived in the same county in Virginia that I was moving from, though we had never met. I think this fact had drawn him to me when we prepared to move.

In his letter, Doug expressed his thankfulness that I was coming to California, and offered his friendship to me, sight unseen. To no one's surprise, when I moved my family to California, Doug and his wife Ruth Ann became close friends. They were the 'spur of the moment' friends whom we could call upon at the last minute to invite for dinner, go out for coffee, for help whenever it was needed.

"I love you, Jim." At first, the words made me flinch. I was almost afraid to hear them spoken to me in this context, by this person. But through the years, these words . . . have become an oasis in the sandy vistas.

Doug, I think, was the first man in my life who would (he still does) say, "I love you, Jim." At first, the words made me flinch. I was almost afraid to hear them spoken to me in this context, by this person. But through the years, these words spoken to me by my friend Doug have become an oasis in the sandy vistas where I usually find myself.

In his book *The Four Loves*, which distinguishes four types of love, C. S. Lewis points out that lovers stand face to face, absorbed in each other by the love they feel. In contrast, friends stand side by side, absorbed in a common interest.[8] Lewis calls friendship the least jealous, the least grasping of the four loves.

Friendship is a love that is easily able to extend to a third and a fourth person, knowing that each will bring a uniqueness of perspective into the relationships. This love is not possessive, not grasping, but more than willing to open up and share. But it is a form of love, and needs to be recognized as such.

What is it about the word *love* that trips men up? I believe men become uncomfortable with the word for several reasons. First, remember that old Saxon word *freond*, from which we get friend. It implies love and freedom. The trouble with the word *love* has to do with the obligation, the restrictions, the commitments of it. To be loved means to be restricted, and men don't like to be restricted. It spooks us in our dealings with women too. We are constantly drawing close, then turning and moving away. Intimacy at once excites and frightens us.

Second, I think we have a very distorted idea of what love can be between two men. Our culture has perverted love and made it synonymous with *eros*, or sexual love, and not the broad definition of *eros* either. Love to us equals *eros*, and *eros* equals sexual love. When two men start expressing love toward each other, it is assumed there must be a sexual attraction.

But the love of friendship has nothing to do with a sexual love, or even a love that possesses. The love of friendship rejoices in the freedom of the friend, and thus lets the friend go continually to grow and become all that the friend was meant to be.

As I can feel safe, reach out in trust to another person, and establish a friendship, I can begin to experience the unique love found in friendship. And as I learn to draw close to another person, to open my life to that person, and be available for that person to open his life to me, my fear of being close begins to dissipate.

TAKE ACTION

1. How safe do you feel with people? Answer the following questions on a sheet of paper.

   Do you find it hard to trust people?

   Is it difficult for you to give/receive nurture and affection?

   Do you find yourself afraid of people?

   Do you often feel taken advantage of?

   Do you have trouble making a commitment?

   Do you find yourself clinging to people you care about?

Do you repeatedly "test" people, expecting they will leave you?

Can you say no?

Have you answered yes to several of these questions? If so, you're probably having difficulty feeling safe with people, which makes it hard for you to connect with people. In the pages ahead, you will find more specific ways to begin to reach out effectively and form relationships with others.

2. Try to notice on television or in other public places people who seem "safer" to you than others. What particular characteristics about each person make him feel either more or less safe? Ask a friend if he can detect in your mannerisms if you are a "safe" person in your demeanor, or an "unsafe" person.

3. Has it been hard for you to say, "I love you" to other people? To your family? To male friends? Can you see the value in doing this?

4. Was love freely expressed (physically and/or verbally) in your home—or was it rarely expressed?

2

WE'RE MADE FOR FRIENDSHIPS

With all our fears—that we can be hurt, that we can't trust others, that we can't say "I love you" or admit we're needy of a person's companionship— why should we pursue friendships? Is it worth the effort? The answer is yes, for a simple reason: We're made for friendships.

As indicated in chapter 1, being made in the image of God means we are made for relationships. Indeed, friendships form the backbone of life, holding us in place, focusing our thinking, directing our activities. Without friendship, life loses a dimension that is irreplaceable. In the following pages we consider just how important close friendships are. We find much help through friendship. Here are four reasons for enjoying friends.

SIGNIFICANCE

In the movie *It's a Wonderful Life*, George Bailey (Jimmy Stewart) stands on a bridge in the snow, lamenting his life. He fears bankruptcy, has had a tiff with his family, and feels useless. He thinks about jumping into the choppy waters below. The predicaments he faces have driven him to question whether he should have even been born.

All of us could have identified with him at that moment. At one time or another all of us have had those feelings. *Have I really contributed anything to life? Would it really matter if I was gone? Does anybody care, anyway?*

Adam missed the paradox, and so have most men and women who followed him: to be fully human, to realize our full potential as individuals, we need to be dependent on God.

The problem started in the beginning of human history, when Adam decided to obtain meaning and significance apart from God. He used the gifts and talents that God had given him to assert independence rather than to acknowledge his dependence. Adam missed the paradox, and so have most men and women who followed him: to be fully human, to realize our full potential as individuals, we need to be dependent on God.

Instead, Adam and Eve used God's gifts for self-validation. The tempter's promise, "You shall be as God" (Genesis 3:4) interested them, and they sought God's glory. As a result, Adam and Eve severed their close relationship with God. All other relationships were distorted at the same time, for whatever affects one relationship affects all relationships.

Man became alienated from himself, and no longer able to integrate his whole being, body, mind, and spirit. Being self-conscious, he saw himself as he was, and condemned himself. Instead of integration, there was dis-integration, and he recognized the sin within himself; it was part of his nature, and he became a slave to sin. Because of his sin, Adam, and all who have followed him, have a perspective on reality that is ultimately contaminated. His cry of anguish resounds through the universe, "I am not significant."

Even as he became alienated from God and himself, man became alienated from others, thus sowing the seeds of social collapse. In the developing social groups (family, community, business, church, even friendship), men and women reflected their

own fallenness and lack of significance. In fact, all of those strategies devised to make people feel significant ultimately failed, and
the individual has felt an increasing sense of hopelessness.

The damage to our sense of reality cannot be overempha-
sized. After the Fall, our view of reality (what is really true) was
contaminated. Perspectives on reality now varied from person to
person, each feeling his perspective was the true perspective. He
was unable to understand that his perspective was limited, or if
he saw it was limited, he could not see that it was contaminated.
People labored under the illusion of certainty, and that "certainty" gave them a false sense of security.

Fortunately, amid the chaos God seized control, and for
those who reached out to Him, He placed His Spirit within them.
This brought about a new sense of identity: "I am uniquely God's
creation." Significance develops as I realize I am God's child.

---

*What are the building blocks of this
new community of restored relationships? Friendships that begin to
mirror here on earth the relationship
we enjoy with God our Father.*

For those of us who have reached out and accepted Christ,
He has entered our being and joined Himself to the essential "I"
of each of us, where the talents, abilities, and gifts reside. He has
begun to reorient our lives according to His true sense of reality.
And as all believers, indwelt by Christ, come together, He creates
a new community, a kingdom of righteousness. This new community begins to manifest the restored relationships that all other
organizations lacked. And what are the building blocks of this
new community of restored relationships? Friendships that begin
to mirror here on earth the relationship we enjoy with God our
Father.

In this new community of friendship, a dynamic interplay
occurs between myself and my friends: we each affirm and re-
affirm to the other what God has made each to be. As the Holy
Spirit interacts with each of us individually, and as I interact then
with my close friends, my internal sense of reality becomes more

and more conformed to God's true picture of reality. I am significant because of a right relationship to God, and because my friends share in my life.

UNDERSTANDING

Friendships help us a second way: we are understood by others and know ourselves better.

Norm and Phyllis were childless. In fact, the doctor thought they would never have children. Then one day, after much prayer, Phyllis became pregnant. The couple rejoiced when a healthy baby girl came into their lives. Lori grew and was a delight to both of her parents. Both scholarly and athletic, she breezed through school. She enrolled in college in a neighboring state and was doing well academically when Norm and Phyllis got the call that terrifies all parents. The call was from the state troopers' office. Their beloved daughter had evidently fallen asleep while driving home for a school break, the car had rolled over, and Lori had been killed.

Norm and Phyllis were devastated. Norm had trouble focusing on anything else than the loss of his daughter. But as Norm related this story to me, when he returned to work a week after the tragedy, his associates there were clearly disturbed by his continuing grief. "Get over it, Norm. It's time to get on with your life," was the recurring message. No one seemed to understand his pain, his utter despair.

From that time onward, Norm and Phyllis decided to dedicate their spare time to helping families who had lost children tragically. Whenever they read in the local paper about a family that had lost a child, Norm and Phyllis showed up at the family's doorstep. They would introduce themselves and explain what had happened to them long ago when they too had lost a child. With sobs of relief, parent after parent would invite them into their homes, and then pour out their hearts to Norm and Phyllis, realizing that finally here was a couple who understood them. Here were people who truly knew the pain.

Friendship is like that. We are given people who understand us. Explanations about ourselves don't need to be long and drawn out. The friend understands.

In addition to having others understand us, with friends we are able to understand ourselves better. It is not good for us to be alone. One major reason we need others is that we do not do well when we "lean on our own understanding." I've seen countless people who have fallen on hard times—marriages have split apart, businesses have gone bad, children have rebelled. For those who have had no one as sounding boards, the consequences have been more tragic.

The reason the tragedy has been multiplied is what has happened in our minds during the crisis event. When we are in crisis, or even when we experience some disequilibrium, our minds have a tendency to magnify the difficulty, or to highlight the wrong aspects, or to see it in a distorted way that leaves solutions all but impossible. It's not necessarily that we have bad minds, we just have minds that need minding, that's all.

Friendship helps us get the understanding we need, and helps us be understood for who we are. For example, I remember a time when I made an error in judgment as I was counseling a family; I needed perspective that only a friend can give. The parents had brought in a young teen-aged girl who was not getting along well with them at home. I had challenged the mother when I probably should have backed off and been more understanding. The next week this mother called to say the family would no longer come in.

I was devastated. *I've let this teen-aged girl down*, I told myself. *She needed me to help her family, and I have not done a good job.* The afternoon after the phone call from the mother, I went to the golf course for a round with my two partners, Rich and Joe. As we played, I explained how upset I was at my tactical error. I still remember how gentle Rich and Joe were with me. They pointed out that I tended to be too hard on myself. They also pointed up other possibilities in my exchange with this woman that I hadn't considered. "Jim, you're not taking into account how the mother acted to block your attempts to help. Also, her husband played a big factor in this with his blatant passivity."

Getting this different perspective from two friends I trust was extremely helpful to me.

Most of us are complex people; we need more than a couple of adjectives to describe us. I know I'm a rather complicated person. I'd like to say that I'm a "tightly wrapped," consistent person who acts and responds completely consistently with all that I believe and value. Unfortunately, this is not always the case. Studies of our brain suggest our complexity.

Remember our discussion in the last chapter of the two parts of the brain? The Survival Brain, we said, deals with safety, and the Logical Brain deals with reason. Actually, the Logical Brain can be broken into its two famous parts, the left and the right brain. The left brain deals with words and logical concepts, neatly dissecting the world into its component parts for careful scrutiny. The right brain deals with the larger picture, creatively beholding the landscape to make sense of relationships and such. Basically, the right side ignores words and logic.

Connecting the right and left sides is trunk of nerves called the corpus callosum. Years ago doctors discovered that severing this trunk reduced the amount of seizures for people with epilepsy. But in the process, these patients also had right and left sides that were no longer in contact with each other. Several patients permitted researchers to run experiments to see how the right and left side respond differently. The findings give us much of our current, popular notions of right and left brain.

> *Friends help you confront the real you. . . . They may recognize and point up your flaws. But friends also help you see your good points, help you get perspective on tough situations.*

One of the most interesting experiments involving these folks with split corpus callosums involved covering one eye. As they viewed the object with the other eye, that side of the brain would be aware of what had happened, but the other side was ignorant of it. (Normally the information would travel across the corpus callosum.)

At one point the experimenters showed the right eye (and right side of the brain) pornography. Upon seeing the pornography, the subjects' faces turned red. These people then were asked why their faces were red. Interestingly, each person had a rational explanation as to why their faces were red, and none of these explanations had anything to do with what had actually happened. They were not logical. The patient would say, "I'm red because I'm hot." Or, "I'm red because my collar is too tight."

That intrigued me. Think about it. At any given time, you or I can give someone a very rational, logical explanation for anything I'm doing, generated by the logical left side of the brain. You can make yourself look noble, or loving, or faithful. It all sounds good. We even believe what the left side of the brain says. (It's so good with logic and words.) The only trouble is, there's a chance that it doesn't match with reality, with what my true values and motives are. In the experiment, the lack of access to the left side (hemisphere) of the brain showed that we could entertain other explanations. We can begin to ask ourselves, *How can we know when our reasoning is correct?*

Friends help you confront the real you. They force you to evaluate your reasoning; they may recognize and point up your flaws. But friends also help you see your good points, help you get perspective on tough situations, give you different angles to consider.

During my five years of counseling in California, I was able to serve on a church staff marked by an unusual amount of healthy friendship and support. What I found, serving with that staff, is that at any given time I had close by many people who understood me, who were willing to participate in my life. They were willing to point out my good and not-so-good points. It was probably the most secure working situation I've ever experienced.

LEARNING THE TRUTH

When I'm kept from the truth, I am vulnerable to believing a lie. Once I begin to believe a lie, I start to act on a lie, and my whole life becomes distorted. Fortunately, friends will tell me the truth.

I was in the midst of wrestling with a tricky contractual negotiation. I had signed a contract to perform a particular service, and in the interim, before that service was completed, I was asked by a competing company to perform a similar service. Nothing contractually kept me from going ahead and performing the same service for the other company. But when the first company became aware of it, officials there were very upset that I would even entertain the thought of working for a competing company while my contract with them was still in effect. True, they said, there was nothing in writing, but this was a matter of integrity.

Was it a matter of integrity? I was unsure. I had never been through an experience similar to this, and in all my reading I had never heard of an experience that matched it. I was truly in a quandary. For I wanted to do what was right, whether or not it was legally correct.

Quickly I sat down and dialed up my friend Pete. I had known Pete for several years; he and I had worked on several work projects together, and Pete knew the specifics of this particular contractual issue. I laid out all of the specifics of the situation as best I could understand them.

"What's most important to me, Pete," I told him, "is that whatever I do, I do it with integrity. I know it's legal."

Pete asked me penetrating questions. We went over the ins and outs of the situation. He pointed out my blind spots. For instance, he told me directly, "You really want to be able to perform this other contract, because it will enhance your name in the community." He helped me pull out my motives and perspectives that I had not, on my own, been able to see. By the time I had finished talking with my friend, I felt as though I had a pretty good idea of the issues and how I as a person figured into what was happening.

One of the great tragedies of leadership, repeated continually in the lives of the kings of Israel and Judah (1 and 2 Kings), is the isolation from people who can tell the leader the truth. Many people don't want to hear it. It seems to them to diminish their power. But Israel's third king, Solomon, writing in the Proverbs, emphasizes again and again the need for strong counsel in a leader's life, so that he can be told the truth. Interestingly, Solomon himself is an example of a king who permitted himself to drift away from the truth as his staff of advisers was diluted.

WELCOMING CHANGE

Friendship changes me. As I make friends, the interaction with those friends changes me. Of course, if they're bad friends, I'm changed for the worse. But if they're good friends, I'm altered for the good.

Clearly, my vertical friendship with God brings about profound changes. As the apostle Paul notes, "If anyone is in Christ, he is a new creation" (2 Corinthians 5:17). Similarly, my friendships with people bring about profound changes. But what are these changes? How do these changes unfold?

Change can be divided into two types: first order and second order. First order changes have to do with minor fluctuations where the rules remain stable. Second order change involves the changing of the rules, a paradigm shift. It's now a whole new game. Obviously, second order change brings about radical shifts in people's basic principles (we are not the same individuals), whereas first order change involves minor variations in behavior (we don't do the same things).

When God comes into your life and redeems you from your sins, He sets in motion the process we call sanctification. This is change on the first order—radical change empowered by the Holy Spirit within you. When your friends interact with you, they recognize a distinct process of change. First, your perspective starts to change. When you become a Christian your whole perspective on life, on yourself, and other people changes. No longer can you see your life as a chance unfolding of cells that have evolved to this place in time that happen to be performing this task now. No, you are made in God's image. You are also His child, and fellow Christians are brothers and sisters. History has purpose and direction. The created order has meaning. You no longer think the same. You no longer act the same.

In the same way, your human friends influence your perspective. They provide new slants on events, ideas about life, and thoughts about yourself that you would not have considered. In those interactions, your life begins to change. You are no longer the same.

Such changes will affect the way you behave in all your relationships (which will cause these people to respond differently to you). A domino effect is produced. Change one individual, and all of those structures, actions, influences, and associations surrounding that individual begin to tumble—they must also change. And this is one of the great benefits of having friends in our lives.

At age thirteen, I was required to take metal shop in junior high school. I shall never forget one particular project. The teacher asked us to make a metal box from a sheet of metal. It could only be eight inches square. After we were finished, the shop teacher had the entire class line up with box in hand in front of his desk.

He then took each box in turn from us as we moved through the line, looked at it, graded it, and handed it back.

My box had some problems. Though the right length (eight inches square), solder had clumped in a couple corners, and the sides didn't fully align. Still, it looked acceptable, if less than perfect. When the teacher saw my box, he took one look at it, threw it into the trash, and wrote an F in his grade book. To a young teenager, in front of his peers, that was devastating. From that point onward, I never thought I could make anything, or work with my hands.

Years later, at age twenty-eight, I bought an old house. The place was basically uninhabitable, but my wife and I knew we could make it charming. Unfortunately, we didn't have enough money to finish fixing the place up. And I was forced to do many things myself.

I can still remember friends coming into that house to admire my work. "You're doing a good job, Jim. Keep at it." As my friends sincerely admired what I was doing, my whole perspective on myself as an incompetent builder changed. Now I realized that I could work with my hands.

Friendships are like that. Once we have friends as part of our lives, we are no longer the same.

TAKE ACTION

1. Are there issues in your life, possible personality traits or habits, for which you have a blindspot, so that you're unable to see these issues clearly? How have you come to be aware of these?

2. Have you ever had a friend confront you with an issue about yourself? Think of the way your friend confronted you. Indicate in your journal how this experience was helpful to your overall growth. (If it was harmful, indicate why.)

3. Think of a friendship that you have had in the past. In what ways were you changed as a person because of this friendship?

3

HOW DID WE GET THIS WAY?

Sam Rayburn, part of a large, poor family in Texas, was ready to go off to college. His parents had brought him to Texas as a small boy after his father, a cavalryman for the South during the Civil War, turned west at war's end. On forty acres Sam's family had struggled to eke out a meager living in farming. Total yearly family income during those decades after the Civil War was twenty-five dollars. His brothers and sisters had all elected to stay on the Texas land and make their livings there. But Sam had other aspirations and had decided to go to college.

Now his father waited with Sam for the train that would take him far away in pursuit of his dreams. Mr. Rayburn reached into his pocket and handed young Sam several bills folded together. They totaled twenty-five dollars. For the rest of his life Sam never knew how his father and mother had managed to scrape together enough money to equal what the family earned in an entire year. As Sam put the money in his pocket, his father put his arm around his shoulder and said the final four words to his son, four words that would echo in his mind for the rest of his life, especially at those difficult times he would one day face: "Sam, be a man."

Sam Rayburn went on to become Speaker of the House of Representatives and one of the most powerful men ever to live in Washington. Today the Rayburn Office Building on Capitol Hill is named in his honor.

And yet, Sam Rayburn was also a man alone. His marriage to a beautiful young woman lasted only for three months. His overall commanding demeanor in the halls of Congress left most people afraid of him. In his private moments, when he was honest with himself, he would confess that the one thing he wanted most was close relationships. And yet he seemed totally devoid of these throughout his life.[1]

To those of us who have been raised male in America, that refrain, "be a man," is a common one. . . . Wrapped in that phrase are all the masculine messages: "Real men don't cry!" "Go on, you can take it!" "When the going gets tough, the tough get going!" and countless others.

To those of us who have been raised male in America, that refrain, "be a man," is a common one. It's a refrain that knows no ethnic, racial, or religious barriers; it seems to penetrate every social and economic class in our country. To hear it, you merely need to be born a little boy in our culture.

Almost every male who hears that simple phrase knows immediately, almost instinctively, what it means. For wrapped in that phrase are all the masculine messages: "Real men don't cry!" "Go on, you can take it!" "When the going gets tough, the tough get going!" and countless others. And in "being men" we push our feelings away (calling them "inconvenient encumbrances").

Lyman Coleman, an author and church consultant, once met with eighteen Presbyterian elders. These distinguished men of the church had gathered in a large circle in a meeting room, and Coleman had posed to the group an interesting question. "Just suppose that it's 3 A.M. and you can't sleep. You have a problem on your heart and mind, and you can't sleep. You know that you can make only one phone call and so you want to call a person who you know would understand, who would listen, who would care, who would be there for you, who wouldn't be upset even in the middle of the night because you've inconvenienced them. Who would you call?"

Coleman directed the responses around the room. The first elder mentioned an old army chum. The second said, "Well, there's a couple of fraternity brothers. I'd call one of them." The third said, "A high school friend who's stayed close over the years." On the elders went, responding around the room until all had finished. Tragically, none of the elders had mentioned anyone in the church where they served, let alone anyone on the elder board who was seated in the circle.[2]

My wife, Marcy, and I sat in a restaurant over breakfast not long ago. Two middle-aged men sat in a booth next to us. For the next forty-five minutes no words were spoken between these two men. They just sat there and read the newspaper in front of each other, together yet alone. These two men are a vivid example of the state of most relationships I witness between men. What has brought us to this condition?

OUR FATHERS' EXAMPLES

Carl was the first in his family to get a divorce. That Thanksgiving he'd gone home to seek advice, comfort, and reassurance from his dad. Finally he was able to corner his father in the den. But when he tried to talk to his father about the divorce, he was shocked when his father walked over and turned on the football game. Carl slumped down in a chair in silence and watched the game with his father. Years later Carl asked his dad why he had been so insensitive at the most painful moment in his life.

"I knew you were hurting," his dad responded. "But I didn't know what to say. So I put on the game, because this was something we'd always done together."[3]

This episode was recounted in a *Parade* magazine article, followed by numerous other examples of fathers struggling to connect emotionally with their sons, finding themselves woefully inadequate to the task. Fathers were rarely present. When present, these fathers rarely knew how to interact effectively with their sons. Communication between fathers and sons was indirect, increasing the possibility of misunderstandings. Misunderstandings led to resentment, which in turn increased the distance between fathers and sons.

Many men feel as though they grew up essentially fatherless. Oh, yes, Dad was there about seven each evening, and we'd hear him rustling out the door early in the morning. On Saturdays he'd be out mowing the lawn. Maybe we'd beg a game of catch with him Sunday afternoon. But as a central male figure, guiding our physical, social, mental, and moral development, that was a different matter.

When men discuss their relationships with their dads, the years melt away quickly, "I starred on my basketball team. Everyone admired me. But my dad, he never came to a game. Never even asked about how things were going." Bill, a self-assured businessman who had found success in the corporate world, was reduced to tears with this long-ago memory. "He ignored me." Tom, an extremely successful auto mechanic, told me, "He absolutely refused to say anything to me, except of course to order me around, to get me to do his bidding. I worked my tail off for him and never got so much as a thanks."

> *A primary reason for limited friendships is the example of our fathers. It is a cycle of uncertainty that seems endless. Fathers don't know how to deal with sons because their own fathers didn't know how to deal with them.*

The anger rises quickly, and centers on the father, the man these grown sons feel knowingly and willfully refused to attend to them when they were growing up.

Under the anger is the pain, the sadness. "I know I let him down. I know I was a disappointment to him." Derek, a college professor of some standing in his community, looked down at the floor. He echoes the themes that have plagued men down through the generations. The anger, the hurt and sadness, the regret. Eric McCollum, writing on the relationships between fathers and sons, points out that the anger comes from sons pointing the finger of blame at their fathers for past indiscretions. The sadness comes from the gnawing belief that something is defective with them, the sons.[4] And what happens to this anger, this sadness that the son feels toward his father? For most of us, it is stuffed down inside. Certainly we rarely express it to our dads. "He wouldn't know in a million years what I was talking about if I was to tell him how I feel."

We became this way—unable to express our feelings and afraid of friendships—for many reasons. A primary reason for limited friendships is the example of our fathers. It is a cycle of uncertainty that seems endless. Fathers don't know how to deal with sons because their own fathers didn't know how to deal with them.

The one place where fathers seemed to rally, seemed to be able to identify and relate, was around baseball, or more specifically, playing catch. It's amazing how most of us can remember nagging our dads until they were willing to drop the paper, go and get their mitts, and come out to the backyard and throw a baseball back and forth. Not only did they throw it, but dads also interacted. They would tell us how to play a sharp grounder, how to get under a fly ball, possibly how to throw a curve. In their time with us, our dads showed that they cared for us and loved us, and we were able, in little ways, to know our fathers better.

But there is always that deep desire to know our fathers better, to dig more deeply into who they are as people. When the movie *Field of Dreams* drew to a close, I saw few men in the theater with dry eyes. Kevin Costner, playing a young man in search of himself, was facing the father he had barely known as he grew up. Finally he is able to force out the words, "Dad, do you want to play catch?"

"Yeah," replies his father. "I'd like that."

And so the feelings dance around in our minds, and there are few solutions as to what it meant to be a son, how now to be a father, and how to broker relationships in the world generally. Our feelings become hidden behind our relentless drive to "make it," to "be enough, get enough," to finally win the approval of fathers long ago dead and buried, of fathers who we thought had drifted out of conscious awareness. We men just bull ahead in the world, grasping for as much recognition, as much hard cash, as big a house as we can get, to mask our pain, to cover the hurt. And of course, friendships don't figure in at all to this equation.

ACHIEVEMENT AND INDEPENDENCE

Society picks up the themes and plays them nicely. Competitiveness is drilled into the male psyche. We should not complain, we mustn't be vulnerable. The slogans are well known: Men Don't Cry. Men Don't Complain About Pain. We Can Take It. Don't Expose Your Weaknesses. Instead, we try to perform and hope we'll be accepted. Slowly, men come to realize that their sense of self is wrapped up in their ability to achieve results. The man focuses more on objects and things, for here he can more easily manipulate to achieve specific goals.

Stephen Covey, a management consultant, points out that in the last generation, our country has shifted from a character ethic to a personality ethic.[5] The character ethic focused on who a man was, his character traits, including integrity, honesty, fidelity, courage, and justice. Now we have shifted to the personality ethic, which focuses on the public image of the person. No longer do we care what is inside the person, but whether he looks good on the outside. So the emphasis has shifted from who a person is to what a person does.

In this environment, men feel pride as they achieve, and especially as they achieve things by themselves. Autonomy, as psychologist John Gray wrote, has become for them the symbol of efficiency, power, and competence. Being independent is the goal.[6]

Consider how men perform as stress is increased. Gray aptly states that as men come under more pressure from problems, they withdraw into their own personal caves and work out their problems alone. In fact, to enter into a man's cave when he is wrestling alone with his problems is to invite trouble. Wives have learned this lesson over and over the hard way. With little success, well-meaning women will offer advice or try to cajole their husbands into emerging to talk over problems (the way women usually do it).[7]

So the emphasis for men has been on achievement and outward appearances over character and personal strength. Personal achievement in isolation has taken precedent over affiliation. That doesn't leave much room for relationships. In fact, relationships become a necessary annoyance. "I need to be with people, but it just doesn't seem to be productive unless I'm striking a deal."

HURTING MEN

As part of an accountability group with four other men, I'd read through a book and then we'd discuss it as part of our time together. One month someone suggested that we read Larry Crabb's *Inside Out*. The women in the church were raving about it, so we thought we'd give it a try. The whole enterprise was a disaster. Viewing the book like a technical manual, none of us (me included) could quite figure out what Larry was trying to get at. It just seemed to all of us like a repetitive attempt by a psychologist to get us to emote. And we weren't buying it.

Looking back on that episode, I now wonder whether the concepts of that book were hitting closer to home than any of us wanted to admit. Larry was digging into our deepest fears, and we weren't ready to let him do that. Author Walter Trobisch once described men as feeling "insecure, inadequate, helpless and fearful, unnecessary and frustrated."[8] This is the reality, but men are left with the image they feel they must uphold. Of course, trouble develops because no one can uphold this image consistently.

But there we are, hurting down inside, with no one to ease our pain. I recently asked a counselee, Greg, to write down some of the secret feelings he had inside. Greg had achieved success in both the military and business after being a star athlete. Everything he did had turned to gold, and his résumé reflected this. But now he dug down inside to reveal to me what was really going on.

"I fear my life's a lie," Greg wrote. "I think that at any time, someone is going to come along and expose me as a fraud."

Men hurt, but they are unable to share the hurt, to reach out and connect with other men to lessen that hurt. One researcher, who has studied men's friendships, has drawn four conclusions from what she observed:

1. Men do not give each other affection. Father stops hugging son somewhere before the boy reaches his teens. From then on, no other man seems to touch the boy much except to give him a firm handshake. Affection is assigned only to the emotional and sexual sphere of life, therefore reserved only for contacts with women.

2. Men do not talk to other men about intimate things. According to the researcher, men will talk with women, or if women

aren't available, to bartenders or in support groups. But rarely do men share what deeply matters to them with other men.

3. Men do not nurture each other. Remember Norm and Phyllis in the last chapter? When they lost their only daughter in a car accident, they were shaken, but Norm was distraught. He had been back to work only a week following the funeral when several of his male co-workers came up to him and said, "Come on, Norm. It's time to get on with your life." Nurture has to do with giving help to those who are struggling. Often this involves a concerned presence and a listening ear. Men don't tend to do this for each other.

4. Men do not have complete and whole friendships. Pogrebin calls these "holistic friendships." By this, the researcher means that male friendships tend to be very utilitarian. The friend fulfills some needed role, nothing more. I wouldn't befriend you just to be with you, to walk alongside of you, to enjoy your person. No, I would befriend you because I needed you for some purpose. When that purpose was fulfilled, I'd drop you as a friend.[9]

THE SECRET HURT

There's a nasty little secret abroad. It's just beginning to peek out from the most unlikely places. No one much suspected it, but you'll probably hear a lot more about it in the next few years. Men have suffered abuse too. Men have suffered much physical, emotional, and sexual abuse as they have grown up. Most recognize and discuss the abuse of women, but few think men have had much abuse. After all, men have never much spoken of that. And many people think, *Well, even if they did suffer, the effects would be negligible, because men are so tough. Right?*

The fact is men have suffered, greatly. And the consequences are just as serious. But they've had even less permission to talk about it than women. So men have packed away all of this suffering, and carried it with them through life, never realizing that the pain has had an effect on their thoughts, choices, behaviors, and attitudes. Many men who are victims of abuse fear relationships and have shut down their feelings in an attempt to protect themselves. Then there inevitably develops the need to be in close relationships. But as these men attempt to draw close, danger signals are activated inside, and they draw away, thus confusing their wives or friends who cannot understand what has happened.

Jack was such a person. When he was growing up, his father had drunk excessively every night before he came home. When he entered the house, he unleashed a torrent of accusing, angry words on whomever happened to be standing there. Once, when Jack's dad had grabbed his wife around the neck in a drunken rage, Jack had stepped between his father and mother. Now Jack found himself in the role of protector of his mom, who usually got the worst of the shouting.

As the relationship between Jack's mom and dad deteriorated, Jack was drawn closer and closer to his mom, who had become very needy and depressed. When Jack's dad was away, his mom would invite him into her bed. Motherly cuddling took on more of an air of romance, and Jack, even as a seven-year-old, became uncomfortable. But his mother's affections toward him increased and became more intimate.

Jack's mother's stroking and inappropriate fondling continued into Jack's teens until he was able to find more and more excuses to be away from the house. Jack took these experiences from childhood and promptly buried them deep inside himself, telling himself that the whole thing was over, forgotten, done with. He never brought this matter up again, to his friends, his wife, or his pastor. But abuse took its toll, and this man drew back from close adult relationships.

Many men look at an abusive past with one of two reactions: (1) "It happened, but it doesn't mean anything and it doesn't matter." This is part of the old grin-and-bear-it school. (2) "It matters a great deal. In fact, I'm a victim and can't be responsible for my actions because I've suffered so much." Both of these extremes get us into a lot of trouble.

Often abuse leaves inside a man much pain; something has to happen with that pain. It doesn't just evaporate into thin air. Some men bury the pain deep inside, so deep that most observers (including the man himself) think it no longer exists. From then on, much of that man's behavior becomes an attempt to keep the pain buried. It's like my having a six-hundred-pound gorilla locked in the hall closet. I don't want anyone to know it's there, because it's embarrassing. I don't even want to remember it's there myself. So I play the stereo real loud when it growls. I spray room air freshener around to quell the stench. I keep the floor outside the closet mopped up and tidy. Now the house has pleasant sights and sounds and smells. *No gorilla here!* I tell myself.

THE LAW OF OPPOSITE EXPRESSIONS

Small wonder men tend to be clueless about how they're feeling. Even if we weren't abused as children, most men still are unsure of their feelings and not willing to express them. That's because as children we were given few tools to discover, identify, and accurately deal with our emotions. In fact, in many of the worst family situations, the expression of feelings was outlawed. (For a good discussion of our fears of expressing emotions, see the first book in this series, *Real Men Have Feelings Too*, by Gary J. Oliver.) Now as adults, when we're asked about our feelings we get funny looks on our faces. We may even go blank for a moment and actually go inside to determine what's there, but we rarely come up with anything significant to say to the inquirers (usually our wives).

In fact, often we say just the opposite of what we mean. I call this the law of opposite expressions. This law confuses almost everyone (though when the law is explained, everyone agrees this "law" is operating all the time). The law of opposites says: "When I'm feeling intensely about an issue, I am just as likely to express an opposite feeling at equal intensity." The chart below shows the law in action.

THE LAW OF OPPOSITE EXPRESSIONS

How I Actually Feel	The Feeling I Express to You
I'm afraid of you.	I berate and attack you.
I feel that you're abandoning me.	I act like I don't need you.
I'm confused and incompetent.	I'm a know-it-all.
I'm vulnerable.	I'm completely in command.
I'm very sad.	I'm euphoric.

The list can go on and on. Unfortunately, men don't know any more than the people with whom they deal that the law of opposites is operating at any given point. In fact, the man himself is usually the last to know that he is employing this "law." That's because men are very poor at identifying what's really happening with their emotions.

The feelings that lie covered underneath are invariably feelings that men are not "allowed" to feel. Men are taught not to feel afraid, vulnerable, and sad. They can only feel in control, confident, and self-assured. Therefore they express feelings of control and confidence even if they don't feel that way. When those "not allowed" feelings of fear and vulnerability begin to emerge, they're shoved back down and the "allowed" feelings are expressed.

Most men, when asked how they feel, get quizzical looks on their faces, and they utter "OK" or "not bad." And then the person who first asked the question goes on as if some legitimate information has just been dispensed.

So it's little wonder that we stumble around as much as we do. Being a man in our culture can be very tough. We hurt, just as women do, and yet we have so few tools to deal with our hurts. We're taught to draw away, to be independent, to reach the top of whatever endeavor we've chosen. And we try to do this. But in the process, we leave friendships behind.

TAKE ACTION

1. Describe your relationship with your father as a child and teen by doing the following on a sheet of paper or in your journal: (1) list specific things your dad taught you as you grew up; (2) describe how he expressed his feelings and what his attitude seemed to be toward showing his emotions; and (3) list the ways of being a man that he modeled for you.

2. What has been your understanding of what it means to be a man? Write a definition below of maleness. Have you found it difficult to live up to the standard of maleness?

   Maleness is: _____

   _____

3. Can you think of specific hurts you suffered when you were growing up? List them on a sheet of paper or in your journal. Then indicate how you have expressed

them since that time by writing down the response (s) that apply:

a. I've ignored them.
b. I've pretty much forgotten about them, suppressing them from my mind.
c. I've told a friend, counselor, or wife about them.
d. I've confronted the person who wounded me.
e. I've forgiven the person who has hurt me.

4

HOW
FRIENDSHIPS WORK

The Bible is a book about friendships. Turn the pages and you'll discover that friendships are everywhere. The most amazing friendship of all, the one that has set the Judeo-Christian tradition apart from all others, is the friendship that God sought to have with the creatures He had made, recorded as early as Genesis 2.

This relentless pursuit by God of people culminates in John 15, where Jesus says, "You are my friends if you do what I command. I no longer call you servants, because a servant does not know his master's business. Instead, I have called you friends, for everything that I learned from my Father I have made known to you." Jesus made a *promise* to us, and because of it we are safe, loved, significant, understood, and not the same. Here's the paradox: as we give ourselves away to His friendship, Jesus makes us more ourselves than we've ever been before.

GOD'S FRIEND, ABRAHAM

Before the coming of Christ, only one man had been called God's friend in the Bible: Abraham. During all those centuries, only Abraham was designated as the Creator God's friend. What a

privilege Abraham enjoyed; this points to the amazing relationship that existed between God and this man. Let's consider what
contributed to his friendship with God.

When God called him, Abram was still a small businessman
in an urban center in the Near East. God made a covenant with
him, and names were changed to reflect the unique relationship
that was unfolding between the man and his God. Abram became
Abraham, taking the name of God into his own name. And God
became the God of Abraham (Genesis 15; 17:1–14). The way
God would describe that relationship from then on was by desig-
nating Abraham as His friend. (Isaiah 41:8; James 2:23)

Now we all have the potential of being God's friend, and that
friendship is based once again on a covenant, a new covenant that
was sealed with the blood of the Perfect Lamb, Jesus the Messiah.
Our friendship with God is made possible because of the character of God. He is the God of love. The New Testament writers
searched for the right word to express this special love and came
up with a seldom-used Greek word, so that there would be no
misunderstanding. The word is *agape.*

This special love springs from the heart of the Lover, and
had absolutely nothing to do with the lovability of the person who
is loved. It cannot, for the person being loved isn't lovable! The
love is without any conditions; it's given freely. That is the love
God offers in a special friendship with Him.

But the Bible also narrates strong friendships between people. Think of the relationship between Naomi and Ruth, a friendship that caused Ruth to leave her family, home, and future to be
with her friend. She chose friendship with her mother-in-law in a
strange land instead of staying in her native land, Moab. Or consider the friendship between Paul and Barnabas that almost ended in a bitter fight. They spent months together in a missionary
trip that brought hardship and persecution along with spiritual
salvation of many they met.

Of course, the friendship between David and Jonathan is the
most often cited in Scripture. Though significant to these two men,
the friendship seems unusual to us modern men who view it over
the centuries. From all outward appearances, this was an unlikely
relationship. Here was Jonathan, heir to the throne, and the man
who would be his chief rival to that throne, David. But for some
unknown reason there is an immediate attraction between these

two men. In some ways, modern Western men have been conditioned to suspect the relationship from the beginning. It has sexual overtones to it, we think. "Could these men have been gay?"

Unfortunately we have difficulty in the modern West allowing two men to be completely heterosexual yet able to draw very close to each other in a deep, abiding friendship. Yet the two men, completely captivated by women in the realm of *eros* (that was proven over and over again in David's life), could embrace one another and give to each other in a wholesome, full love. Their relationship, like that of Ruth and Naomi, contains several elements of friendship.

THE ELEMENTS OF FRIENDSHIP

Let's look at the elements that make up friendship. In looking at the list, you will be disappointed if you are looking primarily for skills, or special knowledge, or any kind of behavior primarily. For as we consider friendship, we will be focusing on who we are as people. Elements of character are much more important than elements of action. What we do is secondary in friendship, for our actions will always flow from the heart outward.

Friendship Starts with a Promise

Bill, an officer in the army reserve, was called to active duty in 1991 once Operation Desert Storm began. He was about to be shipped overseas to the Middle East. Before he left he kissed his wife good-bye, then turned to his best friend Tom, "You take care of her and the children, please Tom. I'm counting on you."

Bill and Tom had been friends since childhood. They had gone to the same schools, played together on sports teams, even attended university together. When Bill and Darlene were married, Tom, of course, was best man. Now Bill would be far away in a combat zone, and he wanted his best friend Tom to look out for his wife and two children.

After several months in Saudi Arabia, Bill noticed his wife's letters were different. No longer were they intimate and reassuring. They contained fewer pages and fewer references to love and affection. Finally Bill's mother wrote to say that Darlene was coming around to her house much less often, and when she did she was much more distant. The month before Bill was to return home, he got a letter he had always secretly dreaded. It began:

Dear Bill,

I hate to have to write and tell you this, but Tom and I are in
love. We have decided that we want to be married. I have already
contacted my attorney and have begun divorce proceedings. I didn't
want to shock you when you got home, and I know you'll be home
soon. So I'm writing you now to let you get used to the idea.

Bill was shattered. It felt like a double betrayal: his wife and
his best friend. All of his props were kicked out from under him.
He couldn't quite seem to get out of his mind the one thought
toward his wife that continued to race around: *How could you?
You promised!* Their marriage was a promise to live together and
honor each other. What had happened to the promise?

A promise is a good place to start in true friendships. This is
where David and Jonathan begin, with a promise. When Jonathan
and David are attracted to each other in friendship, they decide to
make a covenant with each other (1 Samuel 18:1–4).

A covenant is a formal promise. Promises are critical to relationships of all kinds because they are the foundation that holds
all relationships together. You may not have even noticed, but
there's an unspoken promise that is at the basis of even the most
mundane of all relationships.

What is a promise? A promise is a declaration that you will
or won't do something; you declare your intentions. Professor
Lewis Smedes states that when we promise, we obligate ourselves; we bind ourselves to the promises and to those with whom
we promise. If I make a promise with you I've obligated myself
and you at the same time to certain conditions. Smedes says that
the promise is future oriented. With the promise we reach into
the future and bring certainty into an uncertain and chaotic
world. ("I'll be there at noon for lunch. You can count on it!")[1]

This all sounds very formal, and there are formal promises,
which we call covenants and contracts. I believe that the more
we have personally at stake in a promise, the more formal the
promise happens to be. For instance, if I sell you my bike, I just
ask for a few dollars and leave it at that. If I sell you my house, the
contractual promise is very formal and takes a lot of time to draw
up.

When the ancient Jews made formal covenants with each
other, the ceremony was quite elaborate with the splitting of a
sheep, the swearing of vows, the exchange of gifts, the changing

of names, and the cutting of the palms so that blood from both parties could mingle together. This is probably what happened between David and Jonathan. In covenant friendship they and their families were bound to one another. David's enemies became Jonathan's enemies. Jonathan's wealth became David's wealth.

Most friendships are of this informal promise variety. We make friends with each other never spelling out our expectations and obligations. Our differing expectations lead us down different paths, and we end up disappointing each other when our hopes are not met.

Covenant promises are also informally made in the most mundane of circumstances. Even when I'm talking to the check-out person in the supermarket, there are informal promises between us. (The clerk will check out my groceries. I will stand here quietly and not bother her. She will say one or two pleasantries, nothing else, and so forth.) You know these promises are in place the moment someone violates them (such as the check-out person talking endlessly about his medical problems when you asked, "How are you?").

It's obvious that the tricky part of informal, unspoken promises is that most expectations remain unsaid. But these promises are no less binding upon us, obligating us to fulfill certain expectations. It's just that you and I, as friends, may have different definitions and expectations of friendship. For instance, you may view it as a casual, get-together-every-now-and-then relationship. Meanwhile, I see it as a profound obligation to be there with you through thick and thin.

Unfortunately, most friendships are of this informal, unspoken promise variety. We make friends with each other never spelling out our expectations and obligations. Our differing expectations lead us down different paths, and we end up disappointing each other when our hopes are not met.

Bonds of Iron

Our society reflects the deteriorating respect for promises. People constantly complain that obligations are not met in business, in church service, in marriage. In friendship, we must remember that we are bound to one another, that at the base of our relationship to one another is a promise.

Friendship Requires Faithfulness

Sam and Lon came from the same state. Each had great political success and ascended to the U.S. House of Representatives. Sam made it to the House almost a whole generation before Lon, being twenty years his senior. In fact, Lon was elected to Congress just as Sam was seizing more and more power. What Lon wanted more than anything else in his life was power. So when Lon finally made it to Washington, he sought out and befriended Sam. Sam was single and had no family. Many in Washington were afraid of him because he was so powerful and displayed a threatening demeanor.[2] But that didn't stop Lon. He invited Sam to his small apartment every Sunday for brunch. He sought out his advice whenever he had the chance. Before long Sam had been won to Lon as a friend.

Then an issue arose, and Lon saw an opportunity to gain national recognition. To get that recognition, however, he would have to betray Sam, his friend and mentor.

Sam was the type of man who was completely faithful to a friend. It was said around Washington that the tougher the fix you were in, if Sam was your friend you could count on him to come even closer to help you. During Lon's initial years in Washington, Sam paved the way for him, and sprung him out of many jams, being a true friend.

But then an issue arose, and Lon saw an opportunity to gain national recognition. To get that recognition, however, he would have to betray Sam, his friend and mentor. Because Lon put the attainment of power above all else, he went ahead and betrayed his friend. In so doing, Lon crushed their friendship. While Sam

54

was faithful, Lon proved faithless at a key point in their relationship. And without that faith the friendship could endure no more.

Faithfulness goes hand-in-hand with promises. For the degree to which you keep your promises determines how faithful you are. You make a promise to me, and you keep that promise. If you keep all your promises, you show yourself to be a faithful person. When we're faithful to our promises, we can be trusted because we are dependable.

Friendship Involves Loyalty

Malcolm Smith, a well-known Bible teacher in Texas, appeared on television and was heard on radio daily. His messages were well-loved and widely distributed on cassette tapes, and Malcolm was invited into many churches to conduct weekend seminars and scripture teachings. Occasionally he spoke overseas.

But then, as Malcolm was studying the Scriptures, he came to a point where he concluded he needed to make a shift in his eschatology (the doctrine of the end times). This shift did not disrupt any of his basic doctrines, which remained strongly evangelical, but now he adopted a new position on when Christ would return and how events leading to His return would unfold.

The furor that Malcolm's new position caused was catastrophic. Churches dropped support. Meetings and appearances were canceled. Malcolm was stunned. But even more than the loss of church support, what hurt Malcolm the most was the loss of his friends. People who had supported him for years dropped away. Some called with angry denunciations. Others just drifted away silently.

In the midst of Malcolm's devastation, a couple he had known since the beginning of his ministry called. "We'd like to come over," George Jackson said. Malcolm braced himself for yet another barrage. Malcolm ushered George and Karen Jackson (not their real names) into his living room and they all sat down.

"Malcolm," the husband began, "my wife and I just want you to know that we disagree with your new position." Malcolm sat silently, waiting for the final ugly words. "But we also want you to know that we are your friends, and we will always be your friends. So we've decided to stick by you and continue to support you. We know you truly love God and seek to do what is right. So we're sure that however you arrived at your new position, you did it with integrity."

Malcolm was stunned speechless. Here were two old friends, knowing he was being abandoned, now coming to pledge their support to him. All three embraced and cried.[3]

Trials that come into a person's life have a way of separating the genuine from the artificial. And so it is with friendship. In order to find out who are truly a man's friends, put him through a severe time of testing and stress, and his true friends will be there. Despite their differences, the Jacksons could not abandon their friend Malcolm Smith. Loyalty requires friends to stick with each other.

In fact, when everyone else walks out, the friend walks in. We choose relationships with people for so many different reasons. Motives lurk under the surface, sometimes out of our own awareness. We cozy up to certain people because they will help us in our career, because we want to be seen with successful people. *These people further my career, can make me feel important, can get things for me that I want but don't have. I want them as my friends.*

But such "friendships" are temporary, and they're only relationships of expedience. In the midst of a world where people use each other for selfish ends, the concept of loyalty stands out prominently. Some would say that loyalty is a primitive artifact, a dangerous encumbrance. Certainly loyalty to the wrong person or cause can be harmful. But in a genuine friendship to someone you trust, loyalty stands alongside of promising and faithfulness. The promise holds the relationship together. The faithful person keeps his promises, and as a result is loyal to the person with whom he has promised. Loyalty is critical to friendship, because as I draw closer to you I am able to be more open and vulnerable with you. I feel safe because I know that you are loyal and trustworthy. However, the more open I am with you, the more I risk being hurt by you; thus I need to know even more that you will be loyal to our friendship.

But as I get closer to you, as I am able to be open and vulnerable with you, the fear of ridicule and rejection begins to rise within me. Then there's the sense of deficiency: "Am I enough?" At this point, many of us want to withdraw from the other person, to run and hide, to reestablish distance and a feeling of safety. How do we overcome this fear? By having a friend who continues, in an increasing fashion, to show himself loyal and trustworthy. This allows us to draw closer to our friend and to increase our vulnerability.

Friendship Is Reciprocal

John was very upset when he came to talk to me. "My friend George is becoming more and more of a problem," he explained. "George has always been somewhat odd. He had few friends; he's underemployed; he's single and constantly frustrated in his love relationships."

John had met George in a neighborhood Bible study and befriended him. But George was a demanding friend. During the weekly study George took up most of the group time "talking about the latest crisis in his life," John explained. George was equally demanding outside that setting.

"My wife and I would have him to dinner. I'd take him to games, or out to dinner, or to see a show. I'd help him figure out his finances, help him sort through his taxes, find an inexpensive place where he could get his car fixed. But the more I helped, the more George seemed to sink down into more problems. I'm frankly wearing out with my friend George, but I don't know what to do.

"I don't know what the guy would do if I stopped being his friend. I don't really think he could make it." John almost sobbed those final words.

I squared around in my chair and looked John in the face, the way I tend to get when I want to say something important with impact. "Can I tell you what the problem is, as I see it?" I asked.

"Sure. Please, go ahead."

"John, you don't have a friendship with George. It's as simple as that." As I said those words, John stared at me incredulously.

I went on to explain. "John, a friendship involves reciprocity, give and take. Sometimes you give to your friend, and he receives. At other times he gives to you, and you graciously receive. In this relationship with George, you do all the giving, he does all the receiving. This relationship model is the one you find in parent/child, doctor/patient, or teacher/student relationships where the energy basically flows one way."

John listened intently. He came back several more times until he was able to figure out what he needed to do to break the dependent relationship that George had with him. I told him to tell George, "George, you are important to me as a person and as a brother in Christ. However, I don't think our relationship is a healthy friendship. You've come to rely on me when you've really needed to rely on God and draw from your own internal resources." We discussed how John could not plan nor lead George's life, and he agreed to confront George.

Several weeks later John returned to report that George had become angry with him, and the relationship had ended abruptly. John and I talked through all that had transpired between himself and George. And John was able to see the mistakes he had made in forging this relationship with George.

A true friendship is reciprocal. Consider again David and Jonathan. Each gave to and received from the other person in a truly reciprocal relationship. In 1 Samuel 14 we find Jonathan attempting a daring flanking maneuver on the Philistines, apparently relishing his military exploits. David, of course, can be seen throughout Scripture doing the same thing. These two men started out on the same footing with each other, and were able to give and receive from one another throughout their relationship together.

To be reciprocal means the relationship has give and take to it, each person from time to time being in a position to give, and at other times being in a position to receive. Yet many relationships I see aren't true friendships, for the relationships are unbalanced, with all the giving coming from one person.

Naomi and Ruth also demonstrate reciprocity in their friendship. In the beginning, Naomi is the strong, competent mother-in-law who is able to give to her daughter-in-law Ruth. But as she suffers multiple tragedies, she returns home a broken, bitter woman. At this point Ruth takes over and gives to Naomi. Ruth now is the strong one who goes out to support the family.

Reciprocity not only involves the give and take around each other's needs, it also involves initiating the action. Have you ever had a "friend" who never called, never invited you to do anything, never initiated your involvement in his life? If you wanted to do something with that friend, you had to initiate the action. I sincerely question this to be a friendship, for friends find that on occasion one initiates doing things, then at other times the other friend is the initiator. There will be balance.

Friendship demands reciprocity, yet keep in mind that many friendships develop out of relationships that do not start out reciprocal. The men to whom I dedicated this book all are much older than I am and were in teacher/mentor positions with me to begin with. Similarly, I've had a number of clients who have developed into my friends after I'd led them in counseling. At other times (as in the case of Ruth and Naomi), one or the other of the friends will find himself in a very needy position, and unable to give much of anything to the relationship. But over the long haul, friendships will involve a give-and-take, and this will distinguish the friendship from other kinds of relationships.

Friendship Means Becoming Vulnerable

Hank had always prided himself on being a self-made man. "I don't need anybody," was his motto as he maneuvered and steered his way to the top of his profession as an attorney. He was known for his ruthlessness in court; "going for the jugular," he called it.

One day he noticed a light loss of energy; he just didn't seem to have the same get up and go he'd had in the past. Though it seemed unusual, he considered himself a busy man and ignored the fatigue. But his wife and finally his mother prodded him enough to see the doctor. The diagnosis of leukemia hit him as he was driving home. He had been very composed and businesslike when the doctor had made the pronouncement. But in the car, when he was alone with his thoughts, he began to cry. The tears streamed down his cheeks, spotted his Brooks Brothers suit, and splashed on his cuff links.

"Why me?" The question kept echoing in his brain.

When he got home, he pulled off his tie as he practically ran for a chair in the den, raised the newspaper in front of his face, and proceeded to read furiously.

"What's wrong, honey?" His wife was upset, noticing his irritated demeanor. Hank didn't answer. He just stared straight ahead.

Hank's attitude to that point was typical of many men. His focus was on career, mixed in with a little time for sports and leisure. *Relationships are appendages,* he thought. *You hang them onto the margins of life to keep things tidy and in order, but they're not a priority.* Hank steered through relationships on automatic pilot, never giving them much thought.

Instead, he focused on tangible things—deals, and money, and cases—things he could measure and feel and count. Relationships could never be quantified. The "payoff" always seemed too nebulous.

But now he was in a fix, and he knew it. And deep down he desperately needed people to be there with him, to help him through this crisis. But he didn't even know how to reach out, even to his wife. She'd always complained that he never needed her for anything, that he solved all of his problems alone, inside. Well, now he did need her, and he needed others too. But what could he do? Where could he start? How could he even form the words?

Probably you have not suffered a life-threatening illness or accident as Hank did. But suppose that were to happen. Who would you call at 2 A.M. to get comfort, words of advice, friendship? Is there anyone who is close to you?

Men are frightened of one another.
We fear most the harsh judgments
of our brothers. Being competent
has been drilled into us. As a
result, it is extremely difficult
for us to reach out to one another,
to be vulnerable, to ask for help.

A key element to friendships is being vulnerable. Most men, however, are afraid to draw near to others and be vulnerable. Ironically, we don't realize our fears nor our distance. Our communication is shallow; all the while we believe that it is deep and meaningful. We go through the motions with other people. We repeat our stock answers:

"How are you?"
"Not bad. How 'bout yourself?"
"OK."
"That's great. Anything new?"
"Nope."

Psychologist Joel Block questioned hundreds of men about friendships and discovered that men are frightened of one another. We fear most the harsh judgments of our brothers.[4] Being competent has been drilled into us. As a result, it is extremely difficult for us to reach out to one another, to be vulnerable, to ask for help. And yet, the true friend is one with whom you can be vulnerable.

Sounds too good to be true, you might be thinking to yourself. *If I reach out to another man for help, I'd better have my other hand clenched into a fist ready to strike if need be.*

A friend who was caught in moral compromise later told me that he wished he had confessed to me his shortcomings years ago. He said he'd thought of it, but couldn't bring himself to tell me what he was doing. The reason? "I just didn't feel I could safely tell you."

But if we are truly friends, we are safe. We're safe because the promise we make to each other as friends, and the faithfulness and loyalty we use to maintain that promise keeps us safe. And yet people are anxious about being honest and revealing what really is going on inside.

We are vulnerable to the degree that we feel safe. And we feel safe to the degree to which people through the years have kept their promises with us. Those who have been severely abused as children or who have had trusts betrayed in the past will find it very difficult to be vulnerable. Yet all men have some fear of being vulnerable. Finding safety in a relationship is essential for friendship. In "Take Action" at the end of the chapter I outline a way to improve your vulnerabilty in a friendship.

Friendship Encourages the Other's Growth

I don't know that I will ever have a friend like Maj again. Maj came into my life thirty-five years ago when I was a pre-teen and he was approaching middle age, a bachelor in the Air Force. He'd already had many experiences over the years volunteering his time with boys and young men, discipling them and bringing them along in Christ. He encouraged me in Scripture memory. He took me to various Christian rallies; he pointed me to various books to read. But more than anything else, he modeled (and still models) what it means to live like Jesus each and every day.

My brother and I nicknamed him "Maj" way back when we first met him, and that name has stuck over the years. Maj has been an important part of my life continuing into adulthood. In countless ways, especially when I was young and impressionable, Maj was there, encouraging my growth and development, pointing the way, modeling the way.

Once Maj took me on a campout; several other boys were to go, but had to cancel at the last moment. But we went ahead with the trip. After we set up camp in the woods, it was a busy weekend. I cooked a meal for us and did several other chores necessary for earning a Scout merit badge. Maj then sat down with me and pulled out his well-worn Bible. "Jim, it's time to go over your Scripture memory." Maj had coaxed me into the Navigators Scripture memory program. Together we had memorized scores of verses. With patience and firmness he had directed me in the whole procedure. Not only did I come away with the verses forever planted in my memory, I gained an appreciation for conciseness, precision, and self-discipline.

Today, after thirty-five years, Maj is still in my life. Whenever I am with him, I still am able to see his gentle spirit, and hear the words of Christ speaking through him as he shares with me. There is no longer any direct teaching coming from him to me. But Maj continues to model Christ to me.

As you may have surmised, each element of friendship builds on the other. Each point is important to be in place so that the next one will follow. I must begin in friendship with a promise (and I and my friend must be promise-keepers). When I have a promise in place, I can begin to trust. I make a promise, and I am faithful and loyal to the promises that I have made. Our friendship is a reciprocal relationship where we can give and take with each other, and find ourselves on an equal footing. Because of all these things I can be vulnerable with you and open myself up to you more and more. And as a result of this, I can grow as a person.

COMMITMENT TO A PERSON'S GOOD

When my wife and I were deciding whether to move from California back to Virginia, the response of our friends was instructive. Again and again, when we asked for advice about our decision to move, our friends and acquaintances said to us, "Whatever is best for you. That's what you need to do." In effect, these very well-meaning people were eliminating all other considerations from our decision process. At times, I wanted to cry out,

"But what about you? What impact will our moving have on you, and your family, and this church community, and the wider communities in which we live?"

In our extremely individualistic culture, each citizen isolates himself from the larger community, writes professor Robert Bellah; the individual draws a circle of close family and friends around where he can be seemingly in complete control. But friendship is more than just nurturing my own lifestyle. Friendship involves me with you in ways that brings something special into both of our lives. Because you are my friend, I am no longer the same. You have contributed to me and helped shape me into something I was not before.

As I think about it, each of my friends has contributed a different piece to who I am. Steve, a brilliant scholar, together with his wife have helped me to think more clearly, to wrestle with issues in a more reasoned way. My friend Tom modeled to me of how Christ is lived out practically in everyday life. Tom just had a way about him that was engaging to everyone. Whereas I would let many people pass on by me in casual encounters during my day, Tom would engage these people, seeing them as being there for a distinct purpose. Butch also has significantly influenced me during much of my life. He's modeled a consistency of study of God's Word over the years. Meanwhile, Ron showed me how to be comfortable with and accepting of everyone, no matter what the size, shape, color, or other differentiating characteristic.

I could go on and on, each friend contributing another piece to my wholeness as a man. Most of these friends probably have been unaware that they were really contributing much of anything to me. If you asked them, they'd probably say that we just "hung out" together. In fact, there's been little intentional learning from friends; it's all pretty much been "caught" as I've watched them model in front of me various characteristics that I have adopted.

Yes, friends spur us to personal growth. Each friend also brings out another aspect of who you are. Ever notice how you act differently with different people? Not that you're trying to deceive. It's just that we are complex people with different sides to who we are as people. So with some friends you may be silly and carefree; they have simply stimulated that side of you. With others you'll be more intellectual, or more serious and introspective, or more charitable and self-sacrificing.

In addition, friends point out our blind spots. I've had friends on occasion point out to me my inconsistencies and my weaknesses. This really helps me spot areas for growth, and I suspect it should take place more often in my life. But people shy away from confrontation.

My friend Joe was not afraid to confront me. I had decided to move to California and assume the directorship of a counseling center. In accepting this position, I was leaving a partnership that had only recently been formed to do counseling back in Virginia. Joe was willing to confront me with the possibility that I had not acted with integrity. I was brought to tears by him, but the issue needed to be aired.

David Augsburger, a Christian professor of counseling, has pointed up the critical need for affirmation of another person in love, and confrontation with the truth.[5] Our tendency is to swing to one side or the other. Either we confront people with the truth, and take no care for the relationship, or we affirm our friend in love, and never dare to confront him with the truth, fearing it will damage or destroy the relationship.

A major characteristic of traditional friendships cited by Bellah is being committed to the good.[6] Friendship, in other words, points beyond itself. You and I begin to realize that it is not just the two of us who are involved in our relationships. In a real way, our families (both now and in the coming generations) and society in general have a stake in my friendship with you.

If you're a typical American thinker, this last point may seem absurd. You're so very much schooled in individualism and taught that you're the master of your own fate that you will probably find it difficult to accept that the things you do have lasting repercussions beyond yourself. But the ancient Hebrews seemed to have understood this much more plainly. They realized that there were important demands placed upon them as a group. They also realized that their behavior enhanced or diminished the group in ways that to many of them, though they accepted it, were mysterious.

As our friendship develops, as I open up to you and become more vulnerable to you, I am able to grow as a person. And as I grow as a person, society becomes a better place in which to live.

I sometimes wonder about David after Jonathan's death. I'm not sure he did as well as he would have had Jonathan lived. Maybe David would have stumbled into those seriously compromised positions whether or not Jonathan was on the scene. But I can't help but think that Jonathan would have made a difference in his life, because Jonathan was thoroughly committed to bringing out the best in David.

TAKE ACTION

1. Being willing to open up and express ourselves is difficult but essential to a growing friendship. Here are four steps to developing openness and taking risks in a friendship. During the next month try to follow these four steps to vulnerabilty. Recognize that most men are uncomfortable at times with being vulnerable, and the temptation will be to draw back. Realize too that becoming vulnerable to another person is a process, and it will take time (maybe several months) before you feel comfortable in opening yourself up to another person.

Steps to Vulnerability

Step 1. Pick a safe person. This may sound rather obvious, but it's not. Many people who have been hurt and betrayed throughout their lives do not know how to pick safe people. They in fact tend to gravitate to unsafe people (because their parents were unsafe, and being with unsafe people in some funny way feels the most natural to them).

If you've had trouble picking safe people in the past, you might want to get recommendations from your pastor or those in your life you can trust. It is best if you already have a relationship with this person, so the things you will next do with him will proceed more naturally than if you do not know him.

Step 2. Ask this person if he would be willing to help you draw close.

Step 3. Pick a time each week when you can meet together with your safe person for an hour. Decide on a limited time (up to six months) that you will meet together, after which you can decide whether or not to continue.

Step 4. As you begin to meet with your new friend, note your thoughts and feelings in a journal. Share these with your friend. Note your reactions as you begin to reveal your feelings, fears, and hopes with your friend.

2. On a sheet of paper or in your journal draw a circle at the top of the page. In the center of the circle write what you consider to be the center of your life—the driving force or core quality. (Before you place your answer there, think about it. Maybe get some honest feedback from your wife or a trusted friend.) Now under the circle make two columns. Head the left column "being" and the right column "doing."

   Under the "being" column list qualities that you now have (for example, trustworthiness, honesty) and those qualities that you need to continue to develop (for example, perseverance). Make each *being* statement a personal sentence. Introduce the qualities you now have with "I am . . ." and those you want to have with, "I want to be . . ." Here are some examples: "I'm loyal to my friends;" "I want to be more noticeably loving to others;" I want to be able to follow through on my responsibilities." Try to be as specific as possible.

3. In the *doing* column begin to list those things that you want to do. You may want to break the listing into things you want to do physically (for instance, lose ten pounds), spiritually (join a small accountability group), mentally (read three books this year), and relationally (write one letter a month to a friend).

   At your first opportunity, read your *being* and *doing* goals to a trusted friend or your wife or, if you're in an accountability group, with group members. The people with whom you share your lists can help you develop and maintain strategies for implementing these goals in the coming months and years.[7]

5

ARE YOU READY FOR FRIENDSHIPS?

Andy is now in his mid-thirties. He has always lived alone in an apartment that his father picked out for him. His father has been central in his life, unfortunately in a negative way, often undermining Andy's confidence in himself. Andy's father constantly said that Andy would never be able to handle marriage, or even friendship. These words, spoken like a prophecy, hung over Andy all of his life.

He confessed that he didn't like the lonely life he led, but he did not know how to reach out, or whether indeed he wanted to reach out. For Andy, there was always that sense that he was incomplete, that something was missing, and that everyone could see that he was incomplete.

After years of turmoil, Andy came to see me. His life epitomized what I have seen in the lives of many men. Their relationships are shallow. Their confidence in themselves is sadly lacking. Indeed, their ability to determine just who that self is underneath their clothing is lacking.

FRIENDS VERSUS ACQUAINTANCES

Are certain people unable to handle friendship because they are not strong enough emotionally to handle such a relationship? A good question. Frankly, I don't know the answer; it depends on how one defines friendship. Defined broadly, friendship is open to anyone; defined more narrowly, friendship involves challenges certain people may not be able to handle. Several components must be in place within each individual before he can be expected to enter into a deep friendship. Put another way, the place to begin building friendships is within ourselves.

Friendships are far more demanding than having acquaintances, those more casual relationships we develop with many people throughout our lives. A friendship is marked by a special kind of love between two people that develops over a lifetime. Clearly friendships require time and much energy. The people involved experience an ever-deepening bond as they slowly learn to open their lives to each other. This relationship involves an honesty and commitment that allows each to challenge the other to ever-greater degrees of openness. Most men look upon acquaintances as friends because they are not able to build beyond the casual camaraderie that men develop at places of work or leisure. Little effort is put into these relationships, and they can terminate as quickly as they begin.

Having true friends requires being able to reach out to other people, to engage those people, establish a relationship, and maintain that relationship over time. For most of us, this seems like a relatively easy and straightforward procedure. But for others, reaching out and establishing a friendship is a frightening proposition. To reach the depths of friendship requires certain prerequisites. Here are seven essentials for a friendship to develop.

THE REQUIREMENTS FOR A FRIENDSHIP

Feeling Safe

What would frighten a person to the extent that he would not want to risk reaching out to others? The answer is easy yet profound: the person who won't reach out doesn't feel safe. As mentioned in chapters 1 and 4, you must feel safe to reach out. But safety is not an either/or proposition. There are degrees of safety. You might feel safe talking sports with someone, but you won't feel safe discussing details of your marriage with that same person.

Perceiving the world as safe enough (obviously the world has many dangerous aspects) permits you to reach out to others. Genesis 2:25 contains that hauntingly simple phrase that sums up so much. God brought man and woman together; they were both naked, *and they were both unashamed.*

I believe that shame revolves around the sense of deficiency and inadequacy. Exposure to others makes us believe "I'm not enough." Deficiency has become a part of our reality, whether it is real or imaginary on our part. Our fear can be expressed as follows: *When you can really see me, and note all of my faults, then you will know how truly inadequate I am. And once you have seen the inadequacies, you will reject me.*

Love doesn't fear being left out. Friendship love can let go and realizes that in letting go the person will still be there. I can rejoice in your successes. I can see you relate in friendship to others and not be intimidated.

Adam and Eve came together in an atmosphere of perfect trust and loyalty, mutually interdependent and both totally dependent on the Creator. Because of their absolute trust, they were able to be honest and vulnerable to one another without fear of ridicule or rejection. In contrast, I am afraid to tell you who I am, for if I do, you may reject what is there. For me to draw close in friendship, I must feel safe so that I can come near.

Ready to Love

The opposite of love is not hate, it is indifference. The indifferent person does not care to reach out. But the person who has experienced true love and is now able to love can experience friendship. But what is love? Clearly a misunderstood word, love finds its clearest definitions in the descriptions Paul uses in 1 Corinthians 13:4–8. Lewis Smedes' helpful book, *Love Within Lim-*

its, analyzes this powerful passage of the Bible, and I base the following discussion on many of Smedes' insights.[1]

Love hangs in there, even to the point of ignoring its own needs. Obviously this requires a focus on the other person. And love looks beyond one's own needs and focuses on the other person, rendering support when needed (because it's just plain kind). Some people are too focused on themselves and their overwhelming sense of neediness. Friendship will not be a part of their lives until they are able to focus on another.

Love doesn't fear being left out. It doesn't hold on tight, but is able to let go. Erotic love is born of need. "I love you because I need you, and I will possess you." But friendship love can let go and realizes that in letting go the person will still be there. I can rejoice in your successes. I can see you relate in friendship to others and not be intimidated (the idea of *freond*, loved and free).

Love has poise. It doesn't need to come on boastfully or arrogantly. It doesn't need to be rude for that matter. Boastful, arrogant people push themselves into our lives (basically because underneath this strident spirit is a sense of unworthiness and inadequacy). A friend doesn't have to push. He's comfortable enough to sit by and wait until invited in.

Love doesn't insist on its own rights. Love doesn't need to be first all the time. I may even forego a claim to my own personal rights, in behalf of my friend.

Love isn't irritable, irritability being the launching pad of anger. Not that we don't get angry. But anger is inspected and properly handled to make sure it stays within godly limits. True love has the power to communicate anger constructively, so that even if I am angry with my friend, it is not relationship-threatening.

Love hates evil. It seeks to drive it out. Love then rejoices in the truth as it breaks through. Love needs the reality that truth brings.

Furthermore, love carries the burdens and sorrows of a friend. Love believes in the friend, its impulse being to trust in rather than suspect the worst of a friend. In fact, love looks beyond the messiness of this present situation, and peers into the future, and brings hope with it. What does it see when it peers there? It sees Jesus, with all the possibilities He brings into our lives now and in the future.

Love doesn't remove the bad things from relationships; it gives us power to endure them. But not only do we endure the pressure, we grow as a result of it. And, of course, love lasts. In fact, it goes on into eternity. And as you love your friend, that friendship goes on and endures.

Some people are so melancholy that they are never able to laugh, to see the world through glasses other than those that are blackened by gloom and depression. These people naturally isolate themselves from involvement with others, and their sadness makes would-be friends hesitant to know them.

"This sounds idealized," you might now be saying. And certainly this beloved passage in Corinthians has a sense of the ideal because ultimately it is God who can love this way. And yet, the principles that this chapter convey to us are important if we are to be able to reach out in love to others and draw them close in friendship.

Respectful of the Other's Point of View

In each element of love described above, the focus moves away from self onto the other person. Friendship is like that. Friendship requires your ability to recognize another's point of view. Of course, it's impossible to be able to perceive the world totally from another's point of view. But you must be able to focus away from yourself, your own needs and wants, to sense when your friend is hurting, to understand that he can have a valid position (even if you don't agree). This means listening to the other person, discussing his position, and respecting the person's point of view even when you may disagree with his conclusions.

Able to Laugh and Have Fun

Friendship requires that both parties be able to have fun. Much of the relationship will center on shared moments of enjoyment and laughter. Fun and laughter bonds people together. It also gives people a focus of activity that encourages mutual involvement.

The person who can have fun has not let daily problems drain every pleasure from life. Even though we live in a fallen world, God in His mercy has given us enough of His grace so that we can still see the beautiful. We can still settle back and let a symphony enrapture us. We can still see irony in the mundane and have a hearty laugh at the absurdities of life.

Some people are so melancholy that they are never able to laugh, to see the world through glasses other than those that are blackened by gloom and depression. These people naturally isolate themselves from involvement with others, and their sadness makes would-be friends hesitant to know them. Thus they cut themselves off from friendship's possibilities. The sharing of good times and laughter, so common to the close bonds of friendship, will never be the experience of these people. Instead, their sadness distances and isolates them from others. To have friends, we need to be able to laugh at life and ourselves, and to be open to play and recreation with other people.

Confidence in What You Believe

To enjoy a deep friendship, we must be certain about our core beliefs yet flexible about the nonessentials. The healthy person takes a bold stand on a few core issues. However, he recognizes his uncertainty about many other issues. Uncertainty can create a feeling of vulnerabilty. Many men who underneath feel vulnerable are afraid of such feelings, even insecure; so they become more certain, even fixed and rigid in their beliefs.

Belief systems permit us to function in a frightening world. Rigid belief systems are employed when the world has become very frightening. However, in defending our belief system, we must move from a defense of the system to a defense of the self.

Some people are certain about everything. In their linear thinking, A always leads predictably to B, then C. Everything is neat, crisp, black and white. These people tend to be unmovable and unshakable. The more crystallized they become in their position, the greater the possibility that they will drive away potential friends. Security comes in having all bases covered. In contrast, the doubter sees questions that pose other questions. This person is the exact opposite to the extremely certain person. The doubter feels unsafe in taking a strong position about anything, thus he is forced into equivocal positions on everything.

But the person who can enter into deep friendship knows what he believes, and yet has enough uncertainty about peripherals to enjoy the give and take that friendship involves. Remember, your friends will be different from you; enjoy those differences.

Comfortable to Take Action

A man should desire to take action and to bring about what he wants to have happen. This goes hand in hand with beliefs. When we believe in something, we usually will be able to act decisively. When we are ready to act decisively, we are ready for friends. Not only do we act decisively, we take responsibility for the actions we take. If harm is done by our actions, we must admit what we have done and seek to make restitution.

Two extremes can hamper us from reaching out to make friends. A man may act with no input or a minimum of input from others. He may act as a completely autonomous person—"I don't need anybody, thank you." If we're too far out on this spectrum, we never need another person to assist us. We do it all ourselves and take all of the responsibility. In such a world, obviously we won't welcome a friend's perspective.

On the other side of the spectrum is the man who is very dependent and constantly seeks the advice of others, never trusting his own instincts to act. He affiliates with people all the time, but that affiliation is always from a one-down position, the dependent person always grasping for help. The relationship is never reciprocal and thus can never be a real friendship.

The proactive, assertive person takes responsibility for his own life and is driven by his core values. The reactive, dependent person takes his cues from how he feels or what conditions around him dictate. His response often is, "I can't do this. It just doesn't feel right."[2]

At the very heart of the proactive person is the ability to make and keep promises.[3] We commit to do something. We muster our energy and resources and set about doing it. Therefore, friendship requires the proactive person who can make and keep promises to others.

Willing to Be Honest

Honesty is essential to a friendship. The honest man knows and abides by the truth. Truth can be a ruthless taskmaster at times, demanding and unyielding. And yet the honest person seeks it constantly, knowing that truth is the only safe refuge for genuine personhood. This honesty is aimed in two directions: You are honest with yourself. You are honest with other people. This can be called congruence, in that the honest person's actions match his words. This is a simple concept that can be difficult to achieve, and we will say more of this later.

Understandably, honesty with others can be used as a weapon. ("Now I want to tell you what I really think of you.") But for the true friend, it is honesty measured by kindness and graciousness (the love mentioned earlier).

Comfortable with Your Own Feelings

Whenever two people draw close together in friendship, they need to be able to handle the demands that such a close relationship accords—that includes emotional demands.

Our emotions spring from responses to four human situations: pain, danger (the anticipation of pain), pleasure, or desire (the anticipation of pleasure). From pain come the emotions of shame, grief, and depression. From pleasure can arise happiness and joy. From danger comes fear, both real and imagined (which we call anxiety), and sometimes anger. Those emotions can actually be experienced locally in the body; for instance, pain in the abdomen, pleasure in the pelvis, fear in the throat, anger in the chest. Indeed, much of our emotional life has to do with responses as our bodies prepare us physically and psychologically to cope with stimuli of all kinds.

It's really not so complicated. Emotions are natural responses we make to the world around us. They occur naturally over the course of our day, ebbing and flowing depending on how our minds perceive the various situations in which we find ourselves. Therefore we should expect them in relationships with others, especially friendships, for here we spend more time with an individual.

Realize that your attitudes affect your experience of emotion. Your attitudes are those core beliefs you hold deep inside, in many cases, far from your ability to rationally scrutinize. Attitudes are laid down by people close to us as we grow and soon become uninspected laws that govern our thoughts, feelings, and ultimately our behavior.

For example, John is taught from a young age that people can't be trusted. It's hammered in over and over by his parents. This attitude relates to John's basic survival, life and death, so it's a very powerful attitude. Along with this attitude come the feelings of fear, pain, and anger. As John comes in contact with other people, he takes a defensive stance, which keeps people off balance. As they act off balance in John's presence, he becomes more fearful, and his basic attitude of mistrust is continually reinforced.

The attitudes toward six common emotions are shown in the chart below. For many men, their attitudes toward emotions are negative (see chart). In addition, many Christian circles have taken a dim view of emotions, viewing them with suspicion and outright contempt. They believe emotions should disappear, or at least be suppressed, when the Holy Spirit leads a Christian. As a result, many Christian men have developed deep-seated negative attitudes about expressing certain emotions.

The man who is able to have friends is in the process of coming to terms with his emotional life. He realizes that he has emotions that emerge at various times in response to the differing situations. He neither denies his feelings nor gives absolute sway to them. But he realizes how much feelings play in his life as a person, and he is able to discuss this aspect of himself with his friends.

EMOTIONS AND ATTITUDES

EMOTIONS	ATTITUDE ABOUT EXPRESSING THE EMOTION
Anger	I will go crazy, destroy others, be destroyed, be bad.
Fear	I'll be helpless, crazy, unable to defend myself, unmanly, weak.
Sadness	I'll die, fall apart, hurt forever, disappear, go crazy, be ugly.
Shame	I'll be seen as limited and not adequate.
Happiness & Joy	I'll be bad, childish, irresponsible; someone will be angry, jealous, punish me; I'll have to pay it back.

Knowing Who You Are

To enjoy a friendship, you must be sure of your identity—emotionally, intellectually, spiritually, physically (separated with boundaries in place). Anyone who is beginning to reach out to make friends needs to have a growing sense of personal identity. Ask yourself: *Who has God made me to be? What are my strengths and weaknesses?* Remember, you are unique, a distinct, worthy creation of God. Of course, this does not mean that you are operating at peak performance according to your unique abilities. That is impossible, and if you waited to reach this pinnacle before reaching out to others, you would be sadly disappointed. But you can assess your strengths and weaknesses realistically to arrive at a sensible evaluation.

You also know yourself compared to other people, that is, you have boundaries that separate you from others. You don't confuse your thoughts, feelings, and actions with those of others. Though that may seem obvious, many people confuse their own sensations with those of other people; such people are not ready for friendships.

Often we select as friends people who reflect parts of ourselves that we do not give full sway. Quiet people select outgoing people. Intellectuals select party people. It's as if we select those people who can complete us.

The person who knows himself realizes what core values rest at the center of his life. From these core values his behavior is shaped into particular habits as he is able to organize his life according to these value priorities.

On the face of it, the question of personal identity seems cut and dried. And yet, as we dig deeper into ourselves, the situation turns more complicated. We have many facets to ourselves, and we do not act truly consistently at all times. In certain situations, we act one way. In other situations we may act totally differently. And it's not just that we act differently. Our whole sense of self can alter depending on the dictates of external circumstances.

But what remains consistent? What is truly the core of our lives? This unfolding question is critical as we enter into friendship. In fact, we continue to answer this question as we relate to others, for it is a question that cannot be answered in isolation.

CHOOSING YOUR FRIENDS

How do we choose who we choose as friends? This question has intrigued me for a long time. I sat down and thought through all the friends I've had, trying to discern a pattern. I don't think we randomly select friends, but why is one more appealing as a friend than someone else?

Murray Bowen, a theorist on family systems, may have a part of the answer. He argues that we are naturally drawn—whether in friendship or in marriage—to certain people, and we intentionally, though unconsciously, exclude others as we make our pilgrimage through life. He argues that each of us has achieved differing levels of emotional health depending on various family factors as we grew up. We naturally gravitate to those people who rank close to us in the degree to which we have successfully become emotionally and intellectually integrated as people.[4]

But there's another angle to this. Often we select as friends people who reflect parts of ourselves that we ourselves do not give full sway. Quiet people select outgoing people. Intellectuals select party people. It's as if we select those people who can complete us, can fit in the missing or denied pieces so that we can be whole people.

The "whys" as to friend selection may not be as important as the fact that we do select certain people, and these people then become important in our lives.

TAKE ACTION

1. What are your attitudes toward expressing your anger and fear? How has your church experience influenced your attitude toward these and other emotions?

2. Prepare an evaluation of your strengths and weaknesses to help you understand your personal identity. When we are aware of who we are we can reach out to enjoy new friends. On a sheet of paper or in your journal mark your strengths and weaknesses in the following areas:

   a. emotions
   b. intellect
   c. spiritual life
   d. physical life

3. Take out a sheet of paper and write down several friends you would consider close to you. Leave enough space beside each name so you can write several words. Now write in several words to characterize each friend (for example, "friendly, loud, talkative"). You can also add things that each friend has added to your life (for example, "Made me more outgoing").

6

FRIENDSHIP
AND COMMUNICATION

Communication is the glue that holds relationships together. In fact, it's like Super Glue, critical to understanding our friends. Communication makes relationship and growing friendships possible. As we communicate with another person, we subtly influence and shape his behavior, and he does the same to us.

Communication then involves all the processes by which people influence each other. Thus, communication is inevitable and unavoidable. At any given time, we are simultaneously sending and receiving, constantly attempting to make sense of what we hear. To be human is to act, and each act communicates to those around me. What I say and what I do are bound together.

Through communication, community and personhood are possible. My communications bind me to others and permit me to make the adjustments necessary to commune with and become close to others. My personhood is also shaped by the infinite interactions that I have with all the people with whom I come in contact.

OUR BRAIN AND COMMUNICATION

This chapter explores how to improve our communication and thus our friendships. We'll begin by considering how the brain affects our communication.

Earlier we discussed briefly the two different parts of the brain, which we called the Survival Brain and the Logical Brain (divided into the left and right side). Interestingly, each part plays a key role in communication, so let's review each carefully to see how the brain affects communication. Please realize from the outset that when talking about the brain, much still has to be left to speculation.

The Survival Brain

Your Survival Brain (made up of the brain stem and limbic system) is always scanning the environment, reading each person you meet, in order to determine one thing: Are you safe? As I mentioned before, Bert Decker, a communication expert, has studied in depth the workings of our Survival Brain (he calls it the First Brain) as it gathers data on people in our world. Much of our discussion is based on his findings.[1]

Your vision is the dominant sense in the Survival Brain. Vision dominates the other senses when it comes to safety. As you look into another person's eyes, you may feel as though you have direct contact with that other person. Someone has rightly called the eyes "a window to the soul." Ever notice how people who make no eye contact or who stare too long into your eyes or whose eyes dart back and forth make you anxious? Your Survival Brain is noting that there might be some danger there. (It may not necessarily be so.) People's eyes communicate fear, sadness, arrogance, irritability, and a host of other feelings that our Survival Brains pick up instantly.

After scanning the eyes, the Survival Brain looks to posture and movement (Is either threatening?), and then to dress and appearance before evaluating the facial expressions of the person. Remember, your Survival Brain is constantly looking for those nonverbal cues to tell it whether people are safe. Its work continues without your awareness (unless you start to think about it after reading this).

Not only does your Survival Brain use the eyes to look for safety, it uses the ears also to listen for safety. It can listen without actually hearing the message itself. That comes later. Your Survival Brain is finely tuned to the voices of others and can pick up subtle mood changes, even by hearing the inflection of only one word. (Notice how much you can pick up about a person's mood by just hearing the tone of "Hello" on the phone.) The Survival Brain listens for tone of voice, rate of speech, and for inflections, all of those qualities that give information about the person's safeness. Voices can be threatening or mild, loud and ominous, or soft and soothing.[2]

Decker describes the Survival Brain as a gatekeeper. In this capacity, it determines which messages will get through and which will not. This concept has rather ominous implications. You might be rejected, and the wonderful things you have to say may never get heard, because the listener's Survival Brain has judged you to be unsafe and has stopped all meaningful communication at this point.

The Logical Brain

After the Survival Brain finishes its work of assessment for safety, and if the speaker is judged to be safe, the higher levels of the brain take over. This area is made up of the cerebral cortex that surrounds the Survival Brain. This is the area of frontal lobes that is usually associated with thinking (a misconception, but because this area is dominate, it gets most of the attention).

The Logical Brain has two parts, the left and right hemispheres. Each hemisphere, or side, of the Logical Brain has its own function. The left side is the verbal side. It is the side that takes in language and processes it in a very linear way to make sense of the verbal messages sent. The left side breaks messages down for analysis and reaches logical conclusions based on the information given. The right side is more of a synthesizer than an analyzer. It does not use logic but is more imaginative and intuitive. Whereas the left side is objective, the right side is subjective.

Once the Survival Brain has determined whether the person is safe or not, the left and right sides of the Logical Brain take over. The left side of this area listens to the message that is spoken, breaks it down for analysis, and makes a determination of what to do about the message based on logical deduction. It looks at the content of the message. The right side synthesizes all the messages coming from the Survival Brain, takes into account the circumstances of the encounter with the person, and makes a determination of the relationship that exists between you the listener and the speaker. Therefore the right side looks at the context of the message.

Your right side will analyze and determine the major relationship between you and the other person. The message will be placed into one of three categories:

1. *One-up message.* "I'm in control of you, this situation, and hence, our relationship." It appears the speaker is in the dominant position, the position of certainty that communicates I'm in control of this idea or situation.

2. *One-down message.* "I'm not in charge of you, this situation, or our relationship. In fact, I defer to you because I see you being in control of this relationship."

3. *Equal Message.* "We're on equal terms with each other."

I know it all sounds complicated, but there really are no simple messages. That's why we get ourselves into trouble when we communicate, even when we don't intend to.

Let's illustrate how this all works. A person runs into your office and shouts, "The building is on fire. Get out." Your Survival Brain scans this person visually and auditorially to determine if you can be safe in his presence. In a twinkling your Survival Brain registers, *This person is safe. I'll let his message get through.* The left side of your Logical Brain takes the words coming in from this person and analyzes them according to the rules of grammar and syntax, and instantly recognizes the message to be a warning of fire. At the very same time the right side of the Logical Brain looks at the relationship between you and this person. *Let's see, he's ordering me to do something. So that makes him one-up. But under these circumstances, with a fire and all, he should be ordering me to do something. So I'll go along with what he says.*

You respond by saying, "Thanks for the warning," as you run from the office. We can show this process visually in the chart, "Your Brain at Work" (following).

YOUR BRAIN AT WORK

BRAIN AREA	INFORMATION GATHERED BY	MESSAGE RECEIVED
Survival Brain	Visual & Vocal	*"Am I Safe?"*
Logical Brain		
Right Side	Visual & Vocal	*"What's the relationship?"*
		Either *"I'm in charge,"*
		"You're in charge," or
		"We're equal."
Left Side	Words	*"What did you say?"*

Consistent Messages

Each part of the brain contributes its own important pieces of the puzzle to make a coherent message that is understood and utilized by the listener. Unfortunately, at any point in this process, difficulties can and often do develop. This results in the speaker's intended message being lost by the listener.

How does this happen? Because the Survival Brain and the two sides of the Logical Brain are concerned about different things, each part tends to send off different messages, reflecting the differing needs and observations.

To be consistent, all messages sent need to match each other. If I tell you "I like you," you must also be able to pick up that I like you from my facial expressions, tone of voice, posture, and behavior toward you. If all messages match, then my communication is consistent, or congruent as the experts call it. But it's very easy to become incongruent, where messages do not match. For one thing, our Logical Brains long to weave reasonable messages that make logical sense. The only trouble is, many of these logical propositions don't match with our true feelings about a person or situation. Jesus points up this incongruency when he said, "Why do you call me Lord, Lord, and don't do the things that I say?" (Luke 6:46). The words sound great; they just don't match up to the way I live.

The apostle James points again to our tendency to be incongruent. "What good is it, my brothers, if a man claims to have faith but has not deeds? Can such faith save him?" (James 2:14). The author is not talking about faith plus works. He's talking about faith that works. "I will show you my faith by what I do" (James 2:18). To drive the point home still further, the author concludes, "You believe that there is one God. Good! Even the demons believe that—and shudder" (James 2:19). Faith said without faith lived is incongruent.

When the listener detects
incongruency . . . [he becomes]
uneasy, [and then] he will usually
reject the verbal, logical message.
Instead, he believes the nonverbal
messages contained in facial
expressions, posture, tone of
voice, and ultimately in lifestyle.

Our words and actions are meant to fit together harmoniously. When we are incongruent, our behavior comes apart like a puzzle. Instead of our actions fitting together, they combine disharmoniously, alerting the listener that something is amiss.

What do you think happens when the listener detects incongruency? After the listener has become uneasy, he will usually reject the verbal, logical message. This affirms the maxim, "What you do speaks so loudly, I can't hear what you say." Instead, he believes the nonverbal messages contained in facial expressions, posture, tone of voice, and ultimately in lifestyle.

In his first epistle, John the apostle discusses the need for a congruent conversion. "We know we have come to know if we obey his commands. The man who says, 'I know him,' but does not do what he commands is a liar, and the truth is not in him. But if anyone obeys his word, God's love is truly made complete in him. This is how we know we are in him" (2:3–5). Saying I'm a believer is easy. Living it proves authenticity, that Christ truly is inside. Interestingly, John here calls the incongruent person a liar. Not that he would intentionally lie, though that might be the case. More often, however, the person thinks (in his Logical Brain) that he is converted, but God has not yet penetrated his life.

Being Truthful

Clearly truthfulness in communication is important. Yet in one survey of Americans, 91 percent reported they found it hard to get through the week without lying. Only 31 percent of Americans believed that honesty is the best policy.[3] We live in a world punctuated by untruth. As Christians and as friends, we are called to be people of truth.

Truthfulness goes hand in hand with trustworthiness and reliability, words so critical to promise. I make a promise, it's framed in words, and those words must be reliable. To be reliable, those words must be backed up by my consistent behavior.

We are called to be truthful in what we formally assert and what we imply. Truthfulness seems ever more unusual in a climate of doublespeak, jargon, and bureaucrateze, where concepts are used for particular political ends, or to sell something, or to manipulate us generally.

Why is truthfulness in communication so important to friendship? . . . Lies drive us apart, destroy friendship, and ultimately undermine community.

We are called upon to be faithful to the truth, and in so doing we must be truthful to ourselves and to our friends with whom we communicate. Truth is living and speaking in accordance with what is reality. It involves what I say, and how I live and behave. In short, it is living congruently. The apostle Peter wrote, "If anyone speaks, he should do it as one speaking the very words of God. If anyone serves, he should do it with the strength God provides, so that in all things God may be praised through Jesus Christ" (1 Peter 4:11).

Why is truthfulness in communication so important to friendship? "Therefore each of you must put off falsehood and speak truthfully to his neighbor, for we are all members of one body" (Ephesians 4:25). Lies drive us apart, destroy friendship, and ultimately undermine community. But how can we achieve truthfulness?

Being truthful to myself. As seen in the section above, we must first be truthful with ourselves. Our ability to deceive ourselves is limitless. Our Logical Brains say the "right" thing, while other parts of our brains send off contradictory messages. "John, I really want to be your friend," Bill says. "I really want to spend time with you." But as time goes on, Bill does not call, does not find time for John. And John gets the message loud and clear that Bill really had no intention of being friends.

Our minds also distort the truth to ourselves as a means of defending ourselves against truths determined to be too troubling to handle. As a result we deny, we rationalize, we push our own frailties off on others, in a vain attempt to keep ourselves on even keel. And yet, with all our maneuvering, we end up untruthful to ourselves, and as we communicate with others, our messages relay distortion that others pick up. Living truthfully first involves living congruently, so that what you say matches what you do. A painful but helpful exercise would be to ask some people with whom you are particularly close if they perceive you as genuine. If there is hesitancy on their parts, find out where they think you are incongruent.

Being truthful to others. When we are not truthful to others, we engage in lying. Lying involves words that distort the truth, but that's not the whole story. Innocent remarks and beliefs may also distort and subvert the truth. The intent is critical. We can say words to intentionally mislead someone.

We seem to lie in all sorts of different ways: We lie to protect others, as when we say "I love your dress." Such comments seem harmless. Others are matters of life and death, such as the lies told by Anne Frank's protectors. Most of us who lie would like to cast our lies in noble terms. But it can become very confusing when we have stopped protecting and begun harming.

Then we lie in the interest of ourselves. We can do this out of guilt, or shame, or even greed. But the distortion of the truth is there for our own benefit.

We might even lie to cause harm. People have been known to trick people into ruinous courses of action. Others engage in slander (false witness) when they deliberately distort the truth about someone knowing full well that what they say is not the truth. Down deep in our hearts we might wish evil on another person and allow ourselves to gossip, spreading the worst about that person. What we say might even involve truth, but we know it's used to malign the character of that person, spreading details that no one else needs to know.

We can twist, manipulate, and position reality in creative ways to bring about a particular response. Now we are seen in a more favorable light. Or we might employ selective memory, choosing not to remember certain details. All the while, our minds deny or rationalize that what we are doing is really in everyone's best interest.

Why do we lie? I believe we lie to place ourselves at the center of our own universes. Once we are there, in the center, we will decide what is the proper reality, and what is in everyone's best interest, whether or not it matches with the truth.

The results, however, are devastating. Trust is destroyed. You can no longer depend on me to tell you, and to live in front of you, the truth. The liar is destroyed, all the time feeling OK. He creates a web of falsehood, leading to bondage. And little by little the whole fabric of society is torn apart because people no longer live by the truth, no longer tell themselves the truth, no longer tell each other the truth.

Lies seem to flourish in social uncertainty, when people no longer understand, or agree on, the rules governing their behavior toward one another. As a result, there is even a greater need for truthfulness in the Christian community, beginning with the truthfulness that must be found among friends.

Friendship demands the truth. We are friends; therefore we can count on each other to be truthful. We not only avoid lies ourselves; we seek the truth about our friends and ferret out lies told about them. We protect our friends' reputations. Ultimately, truthfulness is the only way we can maintain any community, any institution.

MEN AND WORDS

We know we need to be truthful people as we communicate with our friends. But there are several other traps that can damage friendship. Consider the ways we men use words, sometimes unintentionally, to confuse messages and hinder friendships.

According to linguist Deborah Tannen, when men talk we usually seek to preserve independence and maintain our status. If you're a typical male, you love to display how knowledgeable and skillful you are. Simply put, we tend to be vitally concerned about being and staying one-up. Men want to be the *giver* of praise, the *dispenser* of advice, and the *provider* of information (all high status). We won't be the receiver if we can help it, for this is low status.[4]

Unfortunately, seeking high status and independence are two activities that will not lead to close friendships among men or between a man and a woman. These are the very activities that keep us in competition with each other.

John Gray, a psychologist who has studied communication styles of men, states that a man's sense of self is defined through his ability to achieve results.[5] As a result, many men are more interested in objects than in people.

When doing projects (and men love to be doing projects), you conduct your conversations rather methodically, step by step gathering information, making formal logical connections, much the way a person would go about doing research. This can hinder your discussion of intimate topics, with your wife for example; you still sound as though you're back onto a project—detached, factual, even uncaring. Furthermore, men pride themselves at doing things all by themselves. When stress is applied, men tend to become even more reclusive, retiring within themselves to solve the problem alone.

Women use language completely differently. . . . While men are slinging words around like tools, gathering and dissecting the world into component parts for study, women are using the very same language . . . to draw close.

When it comes to the listener side of conversations, you probably aren't the best at performing this task. You're always ready to dig into what you're told, offer advice, challenge the speaker. Most men are this way.[6] Seldom do we actively listen, attempting to hear what is really being said. Men lose interest quickly, too, especially when they can't find much of a point to what is being said.

Men talking to men understand all of this. As you discuss business, or politics, or sports (the advance and decline of power), you feel comfortable with each other, though you never seem to get very deeply into each other's lives. That would make you feel vulnerable, and that would not be a good feeling. But friendships with women will suffer.

Women (and your wife in particular) can't figure you out. That's because women use language completely differently. Women tend to be more concerned about connectedness right off the bat. Consensus is key to them, which means they minimize differences and avoid superior positions religiously. Language for them is a way of being close, of connecting, of gaining understanding of another human being. While men are slinging words around like tools, gathering and dissecting the world into component parts for study, women are using the very same language to affiliate with each other, to draw close, to be with each other.

So when men and women talk to each other, understandably the sparks begin to fly fast. It's surprising that men and women get anything meaningful said to each other, ever. Men frustrate women with all of the advice they give. Men drive women nuts when men become easily distracted when women are trying to make a point with men. But men absolutely drive women "off the charts" when men withdraw into silence (which is where men usually want to do their most serious, creative thinking).

Our communication style will also cause difficulties when talking with other men. Men tend to do characteristic things that work against strong friendships with both sexes. Consider these:

1. Men ask fewer personal questions. We see this as meddling into private areas, so we tend to avoid this altogether. However, in asking fewer personal questions, we also tend not to draw close to other people.

2. Men are less likely to respond to the comments of the speaker. Frequently, men make no response at all, or show a minimum degree of enthusiasm. The listener feels that men really don't care.

3. Men tend to give more declarations of fact than women. This drives wives to distraction—*Here comes the voice of authority,* she thinks—but in conversations between men, these declarations tend to limit conversation.[6]

Communication is the glue that holds relationships together, makes them work, and determines their direction. When you struggle with communication and keep it to a surface, utilitarian exercise, you lose out on being able to build deeper, more meaningful relationships that can help you in healthy functioning as an individual.

TAKE ACTION

1. Take some time to become more aware of the unconscious processes that influence communication. As you watch the news in the evening, note which newscasters immediately draw you to them, which repel you. (Don't think of the *content* of what is said; focus on the *way* the speaker is talking.) Why do they attract or repel you? In addition, look at people who are interviewed. Listen to the stories that are told. Note the way people stand, their gestures, facial expressions, tones of voice, and eye contact. If you have never done this before, this should open up to you a whole new world of communication you may not have noticed before. It will also help you become more aware and intentional as you communicate with people.

2. Become more active in listening, and try to limit interruptions and disputes when talking. The point is to understand the talker's point of view. Here are three suggestions for better listening: (a) look at the speaker when he is talking; (b) learn to ask good, penetrating questions; and (c) listen for "unspoken" messages that are conveyed through tones of voice, facial expression, and posture.

3. Pay more attention to the spirit of the conversation and recognize that your signals of attention (gestures, eye contact, for instance) are much more powerful than words in communicating that you are listening and that you care.

7

TWO MEN AND
A FRIENDSHIP

I was ushered into Richard Halverson's office in the Hart Senate Office Building. The building itself was regal and imposing, but Halverson's office was rather humble by the standards of power in Washington, D.C. Dr. Halverson, the seventy-seven-year-old chaplain of the U.S. Senate and former senior pastor of the Fourth Presbyterian Church in Bethesda, Maryland, came out to greet me. A recent illness and subsequent hospitalization had left him weaker than I had remembered when last I had seen him, but as always, he was pert and talkative.

We sat down at a round table, and I propped up a small tape recorder.

"Dr. Halverson, I'm here to talk about friendships, your friendships." I could not have selected a more appropriate candidate to discuss this topic. Anyone who has ever know Dr. Halverson knows how important relationships have been to him. He has built his life of service on relationships, and as I sat there listening to him I knew I was in the presence of a pro.

And so for more than an hour, Richard Halverson and I talked about friendships—what they are, how they may change, and how to develop them into something that lasts. I soon discovered that Halverson had a deep, quality friendship with one man, and several good friendships. His words are worth listening to.

"One of the decisive texts for my ministry was given to me in the early 1940s when I was clearly being led into a discipling ministry with men. There were no books being published on this back then, so I decided to read the gospels and find out how Jesus did what he did. As I read about Jesus as he met and dealt with people, I began to realize that there was no clear 'how to' with these encounters. Every encounter was different because everyone he met was different. Then I realized that he didn't have an agenda. What determined the agenda of each encounter was the need of the person. Love responding to the need determined the agenda.

"Mark in his gospel talks about Jesus selecting his disciples. Mark says it in a very interesting way: 'Jesus appointed twelve— ordaining them apostles—that they might be with him and that he might send them out to preach' (Mark 3:14). The most important word in that text for me was the word *with*. The only way you can disciple people is to be with people."

As I listened, Dr. Halverson gradually revealed his thinking about friendships based on years of experience. He was now talking about discipleship, but clearly Halverson doesn't make much of a distinction in his mind between discipling, mentoring, and friendship. Each is a different angle on the same thing.

"This is the way Jesus discipled," Halverson continued. "He was with people, his love responding to those people, the agenda springing from the encounter and the needs of the people he was with. Most people encounter others already having an agenda in their minds. We're with people only to get our agenda accomplished."

Halverson then told a story of his first months as a pastor at Hollywood Presbyterian Church in southern California. "As I sat on the church platform each week, I'd prayerfully look over the faces in the congregation and trust God to lay on my heart the face of a man. Then I'd try to get to that person after the service.

"One morning I spotted this man, and I got to him as fast as I could after the benediction. I went up to him and said, 'I'd like to spend some time with you.' So he invited me to have lunch with him the following Tuesday at his club downtown. We had an enjoyable lunch beginning at 12:30. We just chatted with each other talking about our families and what was important in our lives.

"At twenty minutes to two he looked at his watch and said, 'I've got a two o'clock appointment and I have only ten more minutes. What do you want?'

"I said to him, 'I don't want anything. I just wanted to be with you.'

"He said, 'Come on, Halverson. I know preachers. You must want something. You want me to do something for the church? You want some money?'

"'Honestly,' I said, 'I just wanted to be with you.' He was silent for a long time. And then he said, 'This is the first time a preacher's been with me when he didn't want something from me.'"

Halverson, Senate chaplain since 1981, recalled a recent conversation with a U.S. senator that says a lot about our motives in friendship—motives to get something rather than to give. The chaplain visited the senator's office, and the powerful senator explained how the office sometimes filled with people who were lobbying for one cause or another. "There were people asking for all kinds of things," the senator said.

"Everyone who gets to you wants something from you, don't they?" he asked the senator.

"Yes," the senator replied.

"To me, this is the antithesis of friendship," Halverson told me. "Relationships are built today in order to get something out of them. In our culture, there is [generally] no giving in relationships. It's all getting. Everyone has an agenda, and some are hidden agendas, which are worse. But everyone knows you have an agenda, and you'll get to it eventually. They keep waiting for the punchline.

"We don't need an agenda.
Nothing needs to happen. Being
with each other is an end in itself."

"It's hard for men to realize they can be with people just for the sake of being with them. That is authentic fellowship as in the New Testament sense. John writes in his first epistle, 'We proclaim to you what we have seen and heard, so that you also may have fellowship with us. And our fellowship is with the Father, and with his Son, Jesus Christ. We write this to make our joy complete' (1 John 1:3–4). The consummate end of God's redemptive purpose in Christ was fellowship.

"Fellowship has become a means to an end in our culture, even in the church. We get together to accomplish some purpose, an objective. You don't get together to be together. But in the New Testament, fellowship is the end of God's redemptive purpose."

Halverson is right, of course, and I listened intently as he began to tie together his points. "So whether it's Doug Coe [my best friend], Mark Hatfield [my friend and former Oregon senator] or whomever, fundamentally we want to be with each other. We aren't with each other only when we have an agenda. But we grasp at opportunities to be with each other. The agenda formulates while we're together. Or we don't need an agenda. Nothing needs to happen. Being with each other is an end in itself.

"I see friendship as being, first, responsibility. I'm responsible for my friends. Second, I'm accountable to my friends. Put another way, I can't live a lie with a friend. He's not a friend if I can be different with him than I am at other times or if I'm hiding something from him. If I'm doing something I don't want him to know, then there can't be a friendship. The relationship has to be open and reciprocal."

Halverson's summary of friendship among men, based on observations that span a half century of church and government life, was ending. Now I asked if he could select one friendship from all that he has enjoyed through his long life—one that would demonstrate how he has lived out friendship through the years. Immediately Dr. Halverson mentioned Doug Coe, though he also explained that he has the same feelings toward a number of men he has known through the years. But clearly his relationship with Doug had been very special for a long time. As Halverson explains, "I grew up with a very low self-image. My father was totally undependable. He was drunk most of the time, and he never supported the family. He and my mother were divorced when I was ten.

"And we were very poor . . . in a North Dakota town where nobody was rich. I didn't have a tie to wear. I didn't have a suit of clothes. In those days you dressed up to go to school. You didn't wear Levis. But all I had was Levis. And during my teenage years I had a very low self-image. I compensated with ego, and profanity, and dirty jokes. This was before I knew the Lord. I was seeking security—wanting to be wanted or needed. I think that's connected with my desire, as I went into the ministry, not to be the number one person. I wanted to be number two man to somebody who was doing a great job.

"I knew many great men years ago: Bob Pierce [founder of World Vision], Louis Evans, Sr. [pastor of Hollywood Presbyterian], Jim Rayburn [founder of Young Life]. I longed to be the number two man to a person of that stature. I wanted to go with him, be his shadow, be his servant, and to uphold him. I expressed this to certain people.

"Finally things came to a head when I stayed up all night with a prominent Christian leader. I expressed to this leader my desire to be a kind of lieutenant, or a support in his ministry. It wouldn't be my ministry, it'd be his ministry and I'd be supporting him in it. And I had a very good feeling about that. I felt that he understood. Other prominent men I knew had not understood this desire when I had expressed it. The relationship for them was always institutional or organizational. I'd have a title, 'Assistant to' or something like that.

"But I felt good about this night I'd had with this Christian leader. We had a good deal of prayer, and I got some good, though small amount of, sleep. I was happy. This was going to be a new relationship. The next morning this leader at breakfast announced to [a group including my wife] that I had agreed to come on the staff of the organization he headed.

"That was like the collapse of a castle," Halverson recalls. He became "totally disillusioned." Here was another man who could not understand nor apparently accept a relationship just for the sake of a relationship.

Later Halverson was invited to Willamette University in Salem, Oregon. Mark Hatfield was dean of students at the time. Doug Coe was a leader on the campus and had invited Halverson to lead a spiritual life week at the school. During his week on campus, Halverson learned that Doug "thought exactly like I thought about relationships. It wasn't that we talked about it. It wasn't that we made a decision. Nothing dramatic happened." But a special friendship was beginning.

"Bill Bright had wanted Doug to come with Campus Crusade. Daws Trotman had wanted him to come with The Navigators. Jim Rayburn had wanted him to come with Young Life. But Doug Coe didn't respond to these institutional invitations to be on staff.

He just wanted relationships. So I would say that the relationship with Doug Coe, rather than being a decision made at a moment in time, was a growing awareness that both of us felt the same way. And at some point in that awareness we began to talk about it. Now it's been verbalized, often, through the years.

"So now we're committed to each other for life. We are friends responsible for each other and accountable to each other."

I waited for Dr. Halverson to finish, then I moved in for clarification. "I don't mean to make this sound artificial, but when did you know that this relationship was special? Was there a point in time?"

"I'd say almost as soon as I realized he felt the same way as I did. But I couldn't believe it, of course, because I had been disappointed so often. I'm kind of embarrassed as I now talk about this, because it sounds as though this was something I had well-formulated in my mind from my birth in Christ. But I didn't. This is something I grew into. This is the path that God has led me in. This is the kind of person I am, because of my background, because of my family, because of my childhood experiences and teenage years. All of these things go together to make me what I am today."

"'Well, just give me a couple of minutes to pack my suitcase, because I'm with you,' [Doug said]. . . . Abraham began to see that Doug had not committed himself to International Christian Leadership; he'd committed himself to Abraham Vereide. When Abraham left, he left."

Doug's dedication to the individual was never more strongly shown than when he first joined the Prayer Breakfast Movement of International Christian Leadership, replacing Halverson, who had become the senior pastor of the Fourth Presbyterian Church in Bethesda, Maryland.

Abraham Vereide and Doug Coe worked together several years, but in his mid-seventies, Vereide had become "very discouraged for some reason," Halverson notes. The three men—Coe, Halverson, and Vereide—and their families were then living in the old Fellowship House on Sheridan Circle in Washington.

"Abraham came downstairs with his suitcase packed," recalls Halverson. "He found Doug and said, 'I've had it. I'm quitting.'

"Doug said back to him, 'Well, just give me a couple of minutes to pack my suitcase, because I'm with you.' And he meant it. That stopped Abraham. He didn't understand this kind of a relationship, but after being with me, and then with Doug, Abraham came to realize at least partially what this kind of relationship was about. Not many people can understand it. But Abraham began to see that Doug had not committed himself to International Christian Leadership; he'd committed himself to Abraham Vereide. When Abraham left, he left."

Even I was impressed with the depth of Doug's commitment, so I asked Chaplain Halverson, "Were there discernible stages to this friendship that you developed with Doug Coe?"

Halverson reflected for a moment, then he spoke. "I don't think there were stages to this friendship. But it is like growing, knowing yourself better and better. In this case, I was knowing my friend better and better."

"You're provoking my thinking now." Halverson repositioned himself in his chair, and I knew he was going to launch into a slightly different direction. "When I first came to Fourth Church, I was under pressure to come up with an organizational chart for the church. I realized that all organizational charts are on a vertical plane, which means that somebody is over somebody, and somebody is under somebody. So you have the chairman of the board, and the CEO, then the board of directors, and so on.

"I refused to chart the organization of Fourth Church on a vertical plane because there was that over/under situation, and I didn't want that. Every staff member that came to Fourth Church had a conversation with me. I told them that we were working with each other. You're not working for me. We're working with each other for Christ. And that was clearly understood. Our staff meetings were relational, not business, most of the time. Business items came in the context of our relationship with each other."

For years Pastor Halverson struggled with this. Finally he agreed to design a vertical organizational chart. "I put Christ at the top, " he explained. "Then the members of Fourth Presbyterian

Church, then the officers of Fourth, then the committees of the church. On the bottom line were the staff, which is where we belonged. We were servants to the servants to the Servant.

"As I struggled with this, I thought of the relationships that Jesus had. He had a special relationship with John. When Peter, at the last supper, wanted to know something from Jesus, he asked John to ask Jesus. John was called the beloved. Jesus took Peter, James, and John with Him to the Mount of Transfiguration, and later into the Garden of Gethsemane. So Jesus had a special relationship with these three that He didn't have with the others. This was not an exclusive relationship, but it was special in ways that we don't [fully] know.

"So I can see this idea of circles of relationships. In the first circle with Jesus is John. In the second circle is Peter, James, and John. The third circle was with the twelve. The fourth circle was with the seventy. The fifth circle was with the 120. The sixth circle was the 500 to whom He appeared after the resurrection. And then the circles with others to the ends of the earth.

"I used to diagram that often on the blackboard. The thing that troubled me was the circle was closed. But what I would say was the relationship Jesus had with John blessed His relationship with Peter and James. And the relationship He had with Peter, James, and John blessed the relationship He had with the other nine. And the relationship He had with the twelve blessed the relationship He had with the seventy, and so forth. But these circles on my diagram were always closed.

"One day I was doing this diagram on the blackboard. When my presentation was over, a man came up to me and said, 'Why don't you make that a spiral?' That immediately solved my problem. Now I start with Jesus at the center. Then spiral down to John. And keep spiraling to Peter, James, and John. And on it goes. The spiral can be infinite, so that the relationships are not closed.

"Now the relationship I have with Doug is not closed. If there is something between us, it affects all the other relationships. People know it."

As true friendships mean we are vulnerable and subject to disagreement, I was not surprised that over the years the two men have had what Doug calls "something between us." I wondered about particular conflicts. "Tell me about a particular storm and how Doug and you weathered it."

"We've had all kinds of storms because we're totally unlike each other. Doug is a rational person. I'm a feeling person. I can lose my temper very easily. This has hurt Doug often. Instead of responding rationally to something I think he's doing wrong, I respond angrily. So we've had all kinds of altercations.

"But we are committed to each other for life. And these altercations can't interfere with that commitment. We understand this, and we're verbal about this. It's just like marriage."

I posed another question, probing to determine their level of commitment. "I know you said that you and Doug grew into this friendship. But did you at any time have a formal agreement, a covenant the way Jonathan and David seemed to have done it?"

"No, there was never a particular moment, though Doug uses this"—Dr. Halverson rubbed his two wrists together—"to demonstrate the relationship. We were slowly just discovering each other. And at some point we began to verbalize the relationship."

Fellowship is not a means to an end, it's an end in itself. When men are forming into small groups, I make it a point to tell them that their primary purpose is to be with each other, not to accomplish some project.

I returned to the issue of the storms of friendship. "Was there ever a major misunderstanding that lasted for some time?"

"No," he said emphatically. "No, never. The commitment is very real to us, and we haven't let a rift come between us."

The nature of the relationship Halverson was describing was so rare that I wanted to glean from it as much as I could. The Senate would open in a few minutes, and Chaplain Halverson would have to be there to issue the opening prayer. I asked a summary question.

"Do you, Dr. Halverson, make any recommendations to other men as they consider friendships?"

"There needs to be an awareness in the church of the critical nature of relationships. As a pastor of Fourth Church I felt my job was to nurture the relationships of the members with each other. So much that we did in morning or evening worship was designed to nurture relationships. For example, there was a point in the service when I asked them to hold hands. We finally stopped that when a man approached me who had a crippled hand. No one wanted to hold it and it was an embarrassment. So we changed this and asked people to touch somebody. 'Think of the touch as a channel through which God can bring blessing to the one you're touching. Now pray for that person you're touching.' I constantly tried to make the congregation aware of their responsibility to each other and for each other.

"All of this fits under the category of fellowship. Remember, fellowship is not a means to an end, it's an end in itself. When men are forming into small groups, I make it a point to tell them that their primary purpose is to be with each other, not to accomplish some project. You study the Bible. You pray. But that's not the primary purpose to be together. You be together to be together. Jesus said that if two or more of you are together in my name, I'm in the midst. A good way to invite the presence of Christ is just to be together. When Christ is there, that can determine the agenda.

Relationship is primary. Everything else is secondary to relationship.

"It's so difficult to get men to meet together. They will ask, 'Why should we meet together? What's our project? What's our purpose? What's our agenda?' I try to convince them to meet together just to meet together. And as they start doing it, it means everything in the world to them. Relationship is primary. Everything else is secondary to relationship.

"Dr. Luke recorded in Acts [2:42], 'They devoted themselves to the apostles' teaching and to the fellowship, to the breaking of bread and to prayer.' Fellowship was as important as doctrine. And that apostolic church, under the pressure of godless government, a barbarian environment, couldn't have existed without those relationships."

Listening to Dr. Halverson, I felt I had struck gold. I couldn't leave this goldmine until I had mined all I could get from him.

Finally I told him, "You've stimulated my thinking so much. It seems that one thing has led to another."

He replied, "That's exactly the way the early church worked. Imagine, they didn't have a hymnal. They didn't have a New Testament. They didn't have any theology—that came with Paul. All that they had was the memory of Jesus. Can't you imagine them as they were together. Someone would say, 'Remember when we were with Jesus, and he said this.' And another would say, 'Remember when Jesus did that.' They all were a part of that memory. And one would remind somebody else of something else Jesus had done. This is the way their times together would be, just remembering Jesus."

It was time to leave, so I stood up to shake the chaplain's hand. I had packed up my tape recorder, and tucked my Day-Timer® under my arm when he offered an unusual analogy. "People are like billiard balls on a table. We bump into each other and ricochet around, when we ought to be like grapes crushed together, out of which comes wine." With that image in my mind, I shook his hand, and left.

My meeting with Doug Coe was even more unusual than a Senate office—he reached me on his car phone. His schedule was jammed, but he was gracious to fit me in before a plane flight later that day. Doug, a Christian leader, works quietly in the background in association with responsible people throughout the U.S. and abroad, encouraging bonds of friendship, reconciliation, and understanding in the name of Jesus Christ. He has devoted his life to friendships with men from many different nations, and it's hard to find a person more dedicated.

As his voice trailed in and out on the car phone, he first explained to me his own slant on relationships. "Theoretically, marriage is the deepest relationship that we can have. Two people become one. Friendship can also have a depth that approaches the marriage bond."

The car bounced and I lost Doug's transmission for a second. When he came back, he continued. "I have found that people with the deepest friendships share a common purpose. And that brings me to my friendship with Dick [Halverson]. He and I early on saw our common purpose was to help each other achieve the first commandment, which was to love God with our whole heart, and then to love our neighbor as ourselves.

"The greatest joy and the greatest pain I have had has been in my relationship first with my wife, and then with Dick Halverson. It has been a friendship that has bound us to one another. This binding has included our families and our extended families. Because we came close in friendship, we covenanted to be together in a lifelong friendship."

There have been times when I thought to myself, OK, I've had it. That's it. *But in a few hours I went back to Dick and got things straightened out.*

I was intrigued that Doug also spoke of the covenant nature of his commitment to Dr. Halverson. Though they had not formally exchanged vows, both men felt the relationship was sealed in each of these men's minds in a covenant promise.

"No relationship remains static," Doug continued. "It must be either getting better or worse. My relationship to Dick has always been getting better, and growing deeper. I'm not saying that we've always moved forward with every step. We've had our ups and downs. But we've learned to work these things out." This point I wanted to probe deeper, so I asked Doug the same question I had asked Dick. "How have you managed the storms that have come up in your friendship?"

"We've had some difficult times together, obviously. We've found that it was best to always work these things out before the sun went down. There have been times when I thought to myself, *OK, I've had it. That's it.* But in a few hours I went back to Dick and got things straightened out. After a few days I couldn't even remember what the battle was all about."

Doug had mercifully left his car and gone to a regular phone in his office, so our conversation now was unimpeded by the recurring static of the cellular phone. I asked Doug about his differences with Dick.

"We are quite different people, in our thinking and strategizing. I'm the kind of person who likes the background. I like working with people one-on-one. Dick is an up-front person. He's very gifted in preaching, teaching, and writing. He's had to wrestle with acclaim. Dick would be at a meeting, at the podium preaching his heart out. He'd sometimes wonder where I was. I'd be in some back room working with people. Sometimes that caused tensions between us that needed to be worked out.

"Dick is one of those people who is very intimate when he is up front preaching to people. People feel very close to him. He has been more insecure in dealing with people one-on-one; however, that's been changing also."

"Where do you think that insecurity comes from?" I asked.

"From his childhood. His upbringing is very different from mine. He had a very dysfunctional family. He had a poor relationship with his father. He grew up with a poor self-image that he carried into adulthood. He had trouble realizing that people liked him and valued him.

"When we were together, he assumed that people liked me better than they did him. No one realized that he thought this way. But they noticed when he drew back from personal contacts. People probably found him to be aloof, when in reality he was feeling insecure."

Obviously Doug knew his friend Dick well, his knowledge and perceptions having been sharpened by their times through the years. He could help Dick, and Dick could help him, thanks to their many times together. Doug now told me about his own family environment.

"My family was very close. I have no recollection of any major problems in my family. In thinking about our backgrounds and how we relate to the world, I guess we have been very different, almost opposite to each other. But because we've been so opposite we've never competed. I think if we were more alike, we would compete. But it's also worth noting that Dick has changed as the years have gone by. So have I. Now if you walk with him down the hall, he greets everybody, the senators, the elevator operator, and everybody loves him. And I find that I'm a little less anxious about being up front."

It seemed the positive traits of each had rubbed off on the other. Friendships strengthen the individual. But there was a trio involved in this dynamic called friendship, Doug said. "To the degree that we have trusted God and trusted each other, God has been able to do great things in our lives.

"We have, however, different personalities, just as Andrew and Peter in the gospels were different. Peter was the up-front fellow. He had the vision and could communicate. Dick is always loving and kind and always shows empathy. Andrew worked behind the scenes. He brought a boy with some bread and fish to Jesus, and thus was the first youth worker. He brought some Greeks to Jesus, and was perhaps the first disciple involved in international work. [I'm like Andrew]. Andrew was usually out circling up the tents, finding people and pushing them into the center. Andrew was the one who brought Peter to Jesus, demonstrating his gift to work personally. Dick was great to bring people to.

"Dick and I have always tried to complement each other's efforts. Jonathan and David are also good examples of this idea. David was more the up front character. Jonathan operated more in the shadows."

Our interview was ending and time would chase both of us from the phone. Doug concluded with a simple but profound thought: "We're still together. That's what counts, and we love one another."

TAKE ACTION

1. You may have a friend similar to Doug Coe or Dick Halverson, someone who has been with you for many years. Think of one close friendship that has lasted several years; then take out your journal or a sheet of paper. Begin to write the story of that friendship: when and under what circumstances you met each other, what attracted you to your friends, and what activities you have enjoyed together.

   Don't try to write the whole story in one sitting. As you think about the friendship over time, various aspects will come to mind.

2. Contact the friend you are writing about and tell him of your project. Ask him to relate special instances about the friendship. Jot his observations in your journal also.

3. Leave several blank pages after you have finished. Return to this story as you and your friend continue to "write" the ongoing saga of your friendship, and periodically write down what has happened recently.

8

FRIENDSHIPS DURING THE EARLY SEASONS OF LIFE

S tuart was ten years older than I and much richer. He'd already been a full colonel in the army, and now he was corporate vice president. But he was friendless and hurting. I couldn't help asking myself, *Why would he want me for a friend? I'm younger and poorer.*

Stuart differed in one other way. He had suffered a crushing loss in his life. His wife and son had been killed instantly in a car accident, and he was left without any family. Up until this time, this middle-aged man hadn't much of a care in the world. Now he was left in a big, empty house, surrounded by memories, trying desperately to sort out his life.

I'd known Stuart and his family for a year before the accident. Now I went to the funeral of his wife and son. Afterward I went over to his house. Eventually we talked, and I offered to get together with him one evening the following week. For me it would be convenient, no great sacrifice, for I would work late that night and could drive right by his house on the way home. Stuart jumped at my invitation.

The next week I was there. Stuart was casually dressed and relaxed. Stuart was always relaxed, even in the midst of tragedy. However, his face showed signs that he had not slept well, dark shading under his eyes and frown wrinkles more pronounced than I had noticed before. He walked me around his spacious house, pointing to the various mementos that had been so important to his family. We went into the room of his son, whose life had been cut short just before he was to marry.

"Look at this furniture," Stuart pointed to a beautiful, new, hardwood bedroom set. "I'd just bought this for him. I got it so he could use it now and take it with him into his new marriage." Stuart lingered and stared at the bed for a few moments.

On the night stand the digital clock was blinking on and off the way clocks do when the electricity has gone off, then on again. I reached over and adjusted it, realizing no one had been in this room for awhile.

We went back downstairs and sat in the family room. "It must hurt real bad," I offered. Stuart thought for a moment, brushed past that comment, and asked, "Can I get you a soda?"

"Sure," I said, realizing that Stuart was not interested in discussing the feelings that were undoubtedly churning inside. Later, after we had gotten together a few times, Stuart was willing to open up and talk more about his feelings of loss and sadness. Not that Stuart broke down in tears at any time, or even was able to dig deeply into his soul. He was not. But he was able to be with me, to share his loss as deeply as he knew how.

For the next year I dropped by Stuart's on the way home from work once a week. It became a habit, and I continued it until he remarried. We usually sat in his family room and just talked for an hour or so. I then moved and lost contact with Stuart, though he was already putting a great deal of time into his new marriage, and we had little time together just prior to my move.

FRIENDSHIP AND THE STAGES OF LIFE

This episode pointed up to me the fact that friendship becomes more or less prominent in our thinking at different stages of our lives, as we confront various hardships, as our lives take on differing complexities.

Why do men shy away from friendships? As noted earlier (chapters 1 and 3), we're afraid and few males have shown us how to develop friendships. But there's something else at work also. The need for friendship seems to ebb and flow as we move through life. At certain times in our lives, we will hardly give friendship a second thought. At other times, the need for friendship will be very prominent.

Most men scrape and claw their ways to the top, manipulating the objects and things in their environment, hurrying to see the bottom line, achieving results. Such, unfortunately, is the path that most men take as young people making their way in careers. But then there comes a shift, a time when things begin to change. This was dramatically stated by a man who appeared in *Fortune*'s list of America's wealthiest people; his estate was valued at more than $500 million. One day he sat down with Walt Gerber, pastor of Menlo Park Presbyterian Church in California, recounted the article, and then made this profound statement: "I have made my way to the top of the ladder, and find that it is resting on the wrong building."

A group of elderly gentlemen were once asked what they would do differently if they could recreate their younger years as they made their way up the corporate, business, or technical ladders from which each had come. Interestingly, not one mentioned spending more time at the office or making more money. Each recognized that in his restless pursuit of his goals, he had sacrificed what he now knew to be of most importance—relationships.

Of course, we must ask the relevant question: If a group of seventy-year-old men were to sit down with a group of thirty-year-old men and tell them that in forty years they would long for deeper relationship instead of being at the top of their professions, would the thirty-year-old men be willing to listen? I fear most men do not believe that reality until it's too late and they are already atop the ladder.

THE SEASONS OF ADULT LIFE

Researchers tell us that during our adult years, we men move through particular stages of development. Daniel Levinson has probably done the most to understand men as they have traversed the various stages of adult life.[1] As a researcher into adult development, he has built on the work of psychologist Erik Erikson, who charted the developmental stages of children, which have become so well known to students of child development.

According to these thinkers, we progress through particular stages of development as we move along life's journey. Men and women differ somewhat in their developmental progress, and here we will look only at men's development. At each stage, men are confronted with certain tasks that must be accomplished. If we successfully complete the tasks, we move to the next stage. If we don't complete them, we become stuck until we somehow manage to get the tasks done.

Each of the stages, or seasons as Levinson likes to term them, has its own particular flavor and distinctive. And yet each also blends with the earlier stages so that there is a sense of harmony as a person grows and develops. And yet, as people become stuck in one or another of the various stages, there is also a sense of disharmony.

During the initial seasons of life, when we are very young, we learn to relate to other people, to trust them, and to draw close to them in friendships. However, that occurs fully only when we are raised in "safe" families where we can grow and mature through the developmental stages appropriately. As we grow older, our abilities to deepen friendships are strengthened until we reach adulthood, when we are able to form lasting relationships in marriage and deep friendship.

When Charlie, thirty-five and a successful businessman, visited me, he seemed to have the golden touch. Everything he touched had prospered but one thing, and that worried Charlie enough to visit me. He could not, no matter how hard he tried, form a deep, lasting relationship with a woman, though he desperately longed to do this. Each time Charlie met a woman who would be an eligible candidate, he'd panic. Yes, he'd take her out, just enough times to realize that she was a good candidate for marriage. Then the panic would set in, and he would back away. This cycle had repeated time and time again all through Charlie's twenties and now well into his thirties.

Charlie is an example of a man who is stuck in a season of life. One of his tasks has been to make a decision about forming a marriage relationship, to develop one, and to start a family. (Granted, not everyone will marry; marriage is a choice. Charlie wants to choose marriage, but can't.) He was stuck wanting marriage, but fearful of intimate relationships.

As I worked with Charlie, I realized that I had to go back to the place he was stuck; that was his question: "Can I feel safe in an intimate relationship with a woman?" Charlie and I talked for some time, and finally he was able to meet a woman, fall in love, and marry her.

King David of Israel is a person who can be followed through developmental stages. We will use his life and the stories of other men to look at the various seasons briefly, so that we can get an idea as to why friendship is important at certain times in life, but is secondary at other times. On pages 110–11 appears the chart "The Tapestry of Life," which weaves together the five adult seasons of life. I constructed this graphic several years ago, and it has helped me look at the whole span of a man's life. You will want to consult it as we look at the five seasons in this chapter and the next.

Ideally, a man's spirituality will impact all four areas of his life: relational, vocational, physical, and mental. Spirituality's influence on a man is hard to gauge, though for a fuller, more balanced life, spirituality should come to influence all areas of his life as time passes.

As we consider the five stages, or seasons, of life, pay particular attention to the stage you're in right now. Think of which areas of your life get the most attention (relational, vocational, physical, mental). Consider which one(s) receive the least attention. Ask your wife and/or a friend for their opinions. You may find that these opinions differ from your own. Think of the role friendship has played in your life as you've moved through these various seasons. Lastly, consider (if you've been through more than one season) how your life and priorities have changed as you've moved through these stages.

Novice Adults (ages 20–30)

We meet David as a young shepherd tending his father's flocks (1 Samuel 16), and from the Psalms we know David enjoys composing poetry. But this is not the type of man we usually associate with poetry writing. He is a dead shot with his sling, and he doesn't give a second thought to charging a lion that is threatening his father's flock. He is a man's man, courageous and energetic to the point of capriciousness.

TAPESTRY

		20-30 NOVICE	30-40 SETTLING DOWN	40-50 MIDLIFE
AREA* RELATIONAL	FAMILY	ATTACH TO WIFE; START FAMILY	SECONDARY	CHILDREN GROWN; PARENTS DEPEND; MARRIAGE CHANGE;
	CHURCH & FRIENDS	LESS IMPORTANT	SECONDARY	MORE RESPONSIVE SERVICE
	WORK ASSOCIATES	I'M MENTORED	IMPORTANT TO ADVANCEMENT	I'M MENTOR
VOCATIONAL	SENSE OF CALL	CHOOSE VOCATION	I WANT MORE	NOW WHAT?
	CAREER PATH	APPRENTICE	JOURNEYMAN	REASSESS
	TIME/MONEY MANAGEMENT	LEARN	PLAN	REASSESS
PHYSICAL	DIET / EXERCISE	PEAK	NEAR PEAK	SENSE DECLINE
	SEXUALITY	PEAK	SECONDARY	CAN I?
	HYGIENE	IGNORE	IGNORING SHOWS	NEED TO MONITOR
MENTAL	ATTITUDES	DREAM OF POSSIBILITIES	LIFE'S COMPLICATED	DISILLUSIONED
	EMOTIONS	ANTICIPATION	ASPIRATIONS; AMBIVALENCE	DOUBT; DEPRESSION
	THOUGHTS	IMPLEMENT DREAM	ADVANCE OR CHANGE	YOUNG / OLD DYING /CREATIVE ATTACH / SEPARATE

*All four areas should be affected by a person's spirituality for balance to exist in these areas and in his life.

OF LIFE

AREA*		50-65 MIDDLE ADULT	65+ LATE ADULT
RELATIONAL	FAMILY	COUPLE ALONE AGAIN	NEW OPTIONS; LOSS OF SPOUSE
	CHURCH & FRIENDS	VERY IMPORTANT	VERY IMPORTANT; LOSS OF FRIENDS
	WORK ASSOCIATES	SECONDARY	SECONDARY
VOCATIONAL	SENSE OF CALL	FINISHING THE JOB	RECHANNEL ABILITIES
	CAREER PATH	MASTER	RETIRE
	TIME/MONEY MANAGEMENT	REDIRECT	CONSOLIDATE
PHYSICAL	DIET / EXERCISE	DECLINE	DECLINE & DEATH
	SEXUALITY	IMPORTANT	IMPORTANT
	HYGIENE	MONITOR	CLOSELY MONITOR
MENTAL	ATTITUDES	INTEGRATION	AWARENESS
	EMOTIONS	UNDERSTANDING	ACCEPTANCE; DESPAIR
	THOUGHTS	ASSIMILATION	REVIEW & INTEGRATION

When the prophet Samuel anoints him as the next king of Israel, David couldn't have been more than a young man in his twenties. Looking at David's activities and energies, he is typical of the "novice adult" season of life, ages twenty to thirty. Impulsive and impetuous, David is ready for anything. His military exploits are tempered by his creative abilities with pen and harp. He slays Goliath and becomes a national hero. Then, as mentioned in Chapter 4, he is ready to reach out and make a friend when he first crosses the path of Jonathan, the king's son.

What first strikes me about David's and Jonathan's meeting and becoming close friends is that both are probably in their young twenties. Many of the traits that characterize other young men of this age are true of David and Jonathan. And yet, many young men of this age do not find the time to form close friendships. For some young men, friendships have been maintained with the same fellows with whom they attended high school and college. But few at this age seem to take the time to build new relationships.

If you are a young man of this age, you are probably exploring the possibilities open to you in adult living. Keeping options open is important. There is a sense of adventure and expectancy as you step out, now newly independent and on your own. Your task will be to create a provisional life plan (it'll be revised on and off throughout life) and take on more and more responsibility.

As the chart indicates in this "novice" stage (mental area), you carry a dream as to what you could possibly attain in life. Armed with this dream, you set out to make vocational choices. As you begin your career path, ideally you have made a realistic assessment of your talents, abilities, and skills. At this time, you will usually find a vocation and begin an apprenticeship that will give you valuable skills and opportunities.

But what of relationships during this time of life? You are first and foremost separating from your own families, from mothers and fathers, and beginning the process of finding a mate. During our twenties, many of us marry and begin a new household; we may also start a family. Of course, some men marry at a later age, and the specifics of the time line are delayed in the "family" relational area. At work there is the camaraderie of peers and associates. At this time, finding a mentor to help us in the world of work can teach us valuable lessons and encourage personal growth along the way.

But if you're like typical young men, the pressures of succeeding, of keeping up with peers, of establishing yourself materially and vocationally in the world, tend to force to the periphery personal relationship considerations. Wives and families, though probably present, don't get much time. Oh, yes, during this phase courtship and later marriage will take a great deal of time and energy. But there's a good chance those concerns will slip into the background as vocational pursuits take the forefront. And friendships, especially deep, lasting friendships, get very little attention at all. (See the summary chart "The Novice Adult, Ages 20–30" on the next page for an overview of this season of life.)

What is now needed is intentional mentoring of these young men by older, more mature Christian men. What has been noted in the new men's movements . . . that have swept the country in recent years is the decided absence of older men initiating younger men into the ways of our culture.

During the twenties the difficulties resulting from poor fathering begin to appear. Verne Becker discusses the tensions he had with his father in his book *The Real Man Inside*. His father was an insurance salesman and kept irregular hours, keeping him away from the family a lot. When he was there, he was emotionally distant. How did this situation affect Becker? "I felt empty, hollow, hungry. I had little sense of what it meant to be a man, and no one to teach me. My peers were for the most part in the same situation as I, and I had no male relatives or other older men nearby to serve as role models. I wanted a deeper relationship with my father, but when I didn't get it, I felt betrayed, suspicious, and resentful, not only of him but of father figures, people in authority, and older men in general."[2]

THE NOVICE ADULT: AGES 20-30

OVERVIEW OF THE AGE GROUP.
1. I need to explore possiblities of adult living and keep my options open. Fueled with a dream, I have a sence of adventure. At the same time, I must . . .
2. create a stable life structure and become responsible.

RELATIONAL
1. I need to separate from my mother and father, get married, and learn how to live with member of opposite sex. Children come along, creating stresses—How do I parent?
2. My job is most important. Family and friends must take a backseat.
3. Mentor. Helps me into adult role, realize my dream.

VOCATIONAL
1. Make vocational choice. Assess talents, abilities, skills.
   Life patterns begin to emerge; for example, risk–taker, stable.
2. Apprenticed in a vocation. Acquire skills, values, credentails in chosen vocation.
3. Learning how to manage time/money on own.

PHYSICAL
1. Body at peak performance.
2. Tend to take it for granted, not work to maintain it.
3. Lots of sexual energy.

MENTAL
1. Having a dream of what I could possibly be in life.
2. Thoughts focus the dream into specific areas for implementation.
3. Emotions spring from evaluation of experience in light of how the dream is being fulfilled. Anticipation.

Perhaps this has been the primary cause of a problem that has been pinpointed by researchers James Patterson and Peter Kim.[3] Summarizing their findings, they have declared males in our society between the ages of eighteen and twenty-five to be the number one American tragedy. They are responsible for most child abuse. They are violent, untrustworthy, and undependable. Other trend spotters have noted this ominous tendency in our young male population, a trend that seems to point to the fact that young men in our society just can't seem to keep promises.

If this is the case, that young men in particular are undependable and unable to hold firm to their promises, what is the solution? I would argue that what is now needed is intentional mentoring of these young men by older, more mature Christian men. What has been noted in the new men's movements, both secular and Christian, that have swept the country in recent years is the decided absence of older men initiating younger men into the ways of our culture.

Robert Bly, a poet and lecturer on men's issues, writes that the old men of a culture in the past actively initiated the young men into the ways of that culture, helping them to break the bonds of their families and assume their positions in the community.[4] Today, however, young men have been cut loose to fend for themselves as best they can; research suggests that they aren't finding their way. The mentor acts as a coach, a guide, a teacher, taking the younger man under his wing to help him make the needed adjustments to the adult world. But probably the most important thing that the mentor bestows upon the young man is his blessing.[5] In return, the young man senses the appreciation and admiration, and finds himself prepared for the treacherous adult world that awaits him.

Leighton Ford, the evangelist long connected with the Billy Graham Association, has made young men a priority in his organization. He has intentionally attempted to link young men with mature Christian leaders to school the next generation in Christian leadership. Such intentional programs will be critical in the future if we are to guide young men in the ways of promise-keeping and leadership.[6]

During my own personal pilgrimage through this phase of life, I was typical of young men who seek to become established in the adult world. I was married at the beginning of this time (age twenty-two) and began having children when I was twenty-five. I also stayed connected to the church and was involved in various ways with church activities all through my twenties. This was a time for me to assess my abilities to arrive at a career choice, which took me from youth work into the professional counseling field.

Because friendships were so important to my family, I maintained close friendships (many of which I had begun in high school) throughout this stage. In fact, the man I worked with in youth work was and continues to be one of my closest friends. He and I bolstered each other through the very difficult times that we faced as peers and co-workers during this period.

During my late twenties, as I was beginning to leave this stage, Sheila became a significant mentor, instrumental not only in connecting me with the professional counseling arena but in directing me as I began my career. Looking back, I feel extremely fortunate that I had my friend Ron, my church community and the other friends this provided, and my mentor Sheila to help me through this stormy time of life. I also was stabilized by my wife, Marcy, and together we faced the challenges that this time held out for both of us.

Settling Down Stage (Ages 30–40)

Most men establish a stable life situation during their thirties; they have connected to occupation and family. During this "settling down" stage, you should be working to establish an anchor for your life, to develop competence in your chosen field, and to "settle for" a few key choices.[7] There is that growing sense that you need to "make it." By now you probably have decided what is important, and have headed "full throttle" in that direction to achieve it.

And yet, if you are not careful, personal relationships again will stay in the background as you throw yourself more and more into work. Deep friendships at this age tend to be a rarity. Certainly, men of this age will have many work associates, but nowhere does there seem to be someone who can draw close.

During his thirties, David was firmly established as king, but he also sought to strengthen his hold on the throne and put down outside resistances (see 2 Samuel). Whenever there is a battle, he's in the forefront. David knows his role now, and what he is to be doing. He throws his full energies into achieving the tasks that he has set before himself. The harder he works, the farther he extends the boundaries of the kingdom, just as the harder other young men this age work, the farther they are usually able to advance. But Jonathan is dead. And there is no indication that David has found anyone to replace him in this close relationship that had nourished both men in their twenties.

There are also tensions during this settling down stage (see summary chart on next page). As Levinson points out, it is difficult to establish relationships of family, friends, and community at the same time that you're hurling most of your energies into advancing careers.[8] The two work at cross purposes, and the area of relationships usually gets the "short end of the stick."

Hal was just such a young man caught in the vortex. Now in his mid-thirties, he had established himself in an international corporation as a "doer." He was sent from state to state to troubleshoot difficult areas where the corporate structure needed fine tuning. His job required that he move frequently. It also required that he stay at work for long hours that often lasted into the weekend.

Hal was married and had two children who would be reaching adolescence in a few years. He had rarely been able to attend his son's ballgames. He had only once seen his daughter perform in a play, an activity that was very important to her. Though he'd show up at church most weeks, he never had time for weekly Bible studies or other church activities. He had no real friends. Hal was typical of this settling down stage of life, trying somehow to balance between the demands of his career and the need for deep relationships, and yet sadly failing to find equilibrium.

Hal's wife was not a constant complainer, but she did point out to him that he neglected his marriage and his relationship to his children. "They'll only be young once." She was also concerned that Hal never returned the phone calls of friends who called to engage him in various activities. Those calls had become less frequent in recent years, but Hal didn't seem to notice or mind.

Unfortunately, Hal continued this pattern into his forties when he ran smack into a midlife crisis. He began to question his entire life, his goals, his marriage, everything. He had no close friends to hold him accountable and to help him position his thoughts and feelings in a constructive context. Therefore his

THE SETTLING DOWN STAGE: AGES 30-40

OVERVIEW OF THE AGE GROUP.
1. I need to establish my niche, anchor my life, and develop competence.
2. I need to work to "make it."

RELATIONAL
1. I ask myself, *Do I want to stay married?* My children take second place to my job.
2. I don't have friends, just contacts.
3. My work associates are the most important. But all contact centers on my job. My mentor drops away.

VOCATIONAL
1. I want to be something more.
2. Dreams must be translated into concrete goals. I need to adjust my dream.
3. A long-range money plan needs developing.

PHYSICAL
1. Physical prowess is still at/near peak.
2. Neglect of earlier years may begin to show.
3. Sexuality takes backseat to other pursuits.

MENTAL
1. Life is more difficult/complicated than I thought it would be.
2. I have aspirations and ambivalence about my direction in life.
3. But I think that I must keep advancing up this ladder, or change ladders.

marriage broke up and at forty-five years of age he was a very miserable man.

At this time of life, there is also the loss of mentoring relationships. A mentoring relationship that was useful during the twenties is no longer tenable during the thirties and beyond. The loss of this vital relationship can be very painful to the young man, who now realizes he is truly on his own in the world. At such a time, deep personal relationships would be most helpful in bridging the gap for the young man settling down into adult life. Unfortunately, these relationships are so rarely in place that the young man must now "go it alone" as he seeks to traverse the stormy seas he will encounter.

As I entered this time of life, I had finished my doctorate and was also finishing working in public mental health. My mentor had switched to being a friend, nothing more. I was now ready to launch into counseling as a fully licensed professional. During this time I established a private practice, first by myself, then with a friend.

The man in midlife will probably find that he has embarked on a personal inventory that has him questioning all aspects of his life.

I now was on my own. I no longer had the support of my mentor and close associates that I had worked with over the past several years. In many ways, I knew now that it was up to me to either "make it" or fail. By now I also had three children, a mortgage, and many financial obligations. In many ways, I realized that I was "on the spot" to perform. If I didn't, the consequences would be far-reaching. At this time I did not have a close association with Christian men by whom I could be held accountable. Spiritually I was on my own, hammering out my relationship to the Lord by myself. In many ways, I was typical of men this age, striving alone to make it in the world.

Midlife Transition Stage (Ages 40–50)

The midlife transition stage can be the most painful for men, for they are still in the middle of their earthly lives. In some ways it is the most tumultuous. Some theorists have described it as a second adolescence, where the questions of identity again emerge. At any rate, one gnawing question confronts a man as he enters his forties: What have I done with my life?

Actually, the man in midlife will probably find that he has embarked on a personal inventory that has him questioning all aspects of his life. He'll ask many of the following questions, questions I have heard so many men use in my years of counseling:

Have I achieved my career goals?
How have I been as a husband? as a father?
What have I contributed to my church? my community? my world?
Which way am I going now?
Will I have made a difference when I am dead?

Midlife, with its ups and downs and endless questions, is a time when close personal friendship is essential. Friends can give us the perspective we need looking back on our life . . . [and] the spiritual support that each of us need to carry on effectively.

For many men, this period turns into a full-blown crisis. Jim Conway, a minister and writer, details his own crisis in his book *Men in Midlife Crisis.* He was a successful pastor with a wife and three daughters, yet he was willing to give his wife every material possession, resign his church, and get in his car and "start driving south."[9]

In this stage, some men will feel that they are "coming apart at the seams." Nothing appears to be worthwhile. Everything accomplished to this point may look to be meaningless. For these men, monumental decisions may need to be faced that could shake the very foundations of their lives. Careers are radically altered. Marriages are discarded. Lifestyles are drastically changed.

During midlife the man looks at the past. He notes how much of his life has been based on illusion, and he attempts to root out as many of the misconceptions as he possibly can.[10] Then the man begins to look to the future; *What am I to do now*? he asks. Not that this midlife period is a time of sickness. In fact, as Levinson points out, the need to reappraise actually comes from a healthy part of the man. [11] But old irrational fears, dependencies, and animosities can also cloud the issues that are raised and turn this period into a troubling time indeed. (See "The Midlife Transition" on next page for a summary of this stage.)

David had a very upsetting midlife period. The whole sordid affair begins in 2 Samuel 11 with a very telling verse: "In the spring, at the time when kings go off to war, David sent Joab out with the king's men and the whole Israelite army." Up to this time, David had led his army. Now he sent it out, and he went up on the roof of his house and got himself into trouble with a soldier's wife. Why did David send, instead of lead, his army? No one is certain. I often wonder, as he was approaching midlife, if he was in the middle of reassessing his role as king, reappraising himself as a military leader, deciding to make changes in his life.

At any rate, seeing a beautiful woman taking a bath occurred at a vulnerable time for David, and he relented to temptation. Part of the midlife inventory involves our physical well-being. We realize that we don't have the same physical abilities we once did. Many will attempt to reassert their old prowess once again.

In his action David sinned, and his life changed forever. This is one of the times in his life when I think he longed for Jonathan to be close. For midlife, with its ups and downs and endless questions, is a time when close personal friendship is essential. Friends can give us the perspective we need looking back on our life, trying to see where we have been, looking forward to what we hope to accomplish, and giving us the spiritual support that each of us needs to carry on effectively.

Friends can also keep us accountable as we consider changes, wrestle with temptations, and slowly begin the process of carving out new opportunities at work, home, church, and in the community. I have been associated with several friends during midlife reevaluations who have sensed God's call on their life for full-time vocational Christian ministry. The friendship was essential in assessing the validity of the call and determining the specific steps needed to fulfill what each friend sensed God was leading him to do.

MIDLIFE TRANSITION: AGES 40-50

OVERVIEW OF THE AGE GROUP.

1. I must review my life and reappraise what I've done with it.
2. I must modify negative elements in my life, and look toward new choices in the future. The old rules don't work any more; I must find new ones.

RELATIONAL

1. My marriage is different. My children are growing/grown, creating stresses of their own. And my parents are now more dependent on me.
2. I've become a more responsive friend to men and women. The need is kindling within me to serve others.
3. I can really get to know work associates, not just compete with them. And now I'm a mentor for the young.

VOCATIONAL

1. There's a gap between what I thought I'd be. and what I am. *OR* . . . I did achieve my dream. Now can I find another dream?
2. Maybe job performance is not the only criterion of my worth.
3. I must reassess the distribution of time/value of money in my life.

PHYSICAL

1. My first sense of decline. I'm not what I was. And I'm going to die.
2. I've got to prove I'm still sexually attractive.
3. I need to monitor myself much more closely.

MENTAL

1. I am disillusioned with my most cherished beliefs and values. I must reassess all I believe in.
2. Doubt and depression.
3. I am young/I am old.
   I am dying/I must create.
   I must be attached/I must be separate.

Jim Conway in his book echoes the critical importance of friends during this time of life.[12] Conway notes that those friends are apt to be in for a great deal of abuse at the hands of the troubled midlife man. He will give excuse after excuse as to why he is unavailable, the ravages of the crisis having taken their toll. But the pressures of this period will also highlight the true friends in a man's life.

My friend Rich went into a midlife spiral soon after I left for California. His struggle called into question almost every area of his life: his values, his marriage, his future. He'd spend long hours composing poetry or sitting on a mountain gazing at the scenery. My other friend, Joe, was fortunately on the scene. I don't think Joe really imparted many words of wisdom during this time. He was just there and available to Rich. He listened to his poetry, heard his struggles about life, and remained constant.

Though still in my midlife years as I write this chapter, I have had my share of questions and life changes. At forty I accepted a call to leave a lucrative private practice in the town where my family has lived for three hundred years and travel to California where I became director of a church counseling center. My friends and family thought that I had lost my mind. To them, the venture seemed all risk with no real benefits.

What had appealed to me the most was the opportunity to do new things, things I'd thought about for years, but never had the opportunity to do. And I realized that if I didn't do it now, I'd probably never get the chance to do it again. So we packed up and moved. Fortunately for my family, God was gracious, and the experience turned out to be very positive for all of us. Now I have moved back to my old practice and have reestablished my ties with church, community, and most importantly, friends.

This experience was instrumental in pointing up to me what things I should emphasize for the rest of my life and what things I probably ought to avoid. As an example, I found I was good at speaking and teaching, but not very good at administration.

One of the most significant anchors in my life, as I progressed through this midlife period, was the presence of friends. Many were old friends I had left behind in Virginia as a ventured to California. Others were new friends I found in California. Both old and new, these friendships were critical to my own stability as I have been traversing this stormy stage of life.

By the time we have reached the end of the midlife years, we have faced many crises, both great and small. We have forged a way vocationally and established ourselves financially. We have settled into family life, learned how to be husbands and fathers, and are well along in raising children. Our physical and mental well-being is predicated on how much time we have devoted to maintaining each area. Hopefully we have also maintained a strong spiritual life which has included close friendships to nurture our spiritual development.

We are now ready for the final two acts to unfold in the stages of life, two acts that will also greatly influence our friendships.

TAKE ACTION

1. If you are still in one of the stages we've mentioned, note where you fall on the chart. Is the chart accurate as to what you are now doing in each of the four areas (relational, vocational, physical, mental)?

2. If you have already completed these stages, did you follow fairly closely the developmental stages here listed? Where did you deviate? What would you have done differently?

9
FRIENDSHIPS DURING THE LATER YEARS

The first wave of Baby Boomers is about to reach the golden shores of fifty. Though it may be hard to believe, those born earliest in the baby boom of 1946 to 1964 will begin to reach age fifty—middle adult life—by the mid 1990s. Many of us will see this golden age much sooner than we think; some readers are already there. Though we endure an obvious physical decline, in our later years our relationships, vocation, and mental development can yield benefit in crucial ways. All this influences our friendships. Let's look at the final two seasons of life.

The Middle Adult Years (Ages 50–65)

The stage known as middle adulthood is a time of maturity but also difficulty. Consider King David; as he entered this time, the tempo of difficulty seemed to increase. His son Absalom turned against him and took several of David's most trusted friends and advisers with him (2 Samuel 15). Absalom's rebellion and subsequent death had a profound effect on the aging David. Just when he seemed to have finished with this, he had to deal with another rebellion in his kingdom. Then, when all seemed to have settled down, David numbered his men in violation of God's command, and found himself once again at odds with the God he'd served all his life.

If you are in this phase of life, you are faced with critical choices and challenges that will set your course for the rest of your life (see summary chart on next page). This is a time when, if you have worked hard and wisely, you are looked up to at work, in the community, and in the church. You are probably financially more comfortable than you have ever been. And yet there are also stresses and strains in your life. You must now finish launching your children into the world and deal with a marriage that is not distracted by children. This is called the "empty nest syndrome" because so many parents feel incomplete when their children leave. Caught off guard when they must face each other, husbands and wives have stress instead of bliss with one another. (Many couples submerge their conflicts as they focus on their children. When the children leave, the conflict emerges.)

If you are in your fifties, the launching of your children may not have gone all that smoothly. As King David had a number of problems with his grown children, many of you may still be struggling with children who are now grown but who, for various reasons, still maintain negative contact with you and your wife.

At this time friendship for many men becomes extremely important. There are no more corporate ladders to climb, no more financial or political dragons to slay. As you catch your breath, you may . . . look around and find that you have no friends. . .

You may also be called upon to care for your aging parents. This role reversal, where your parents now depend on you for their care, can be very difficult for some men, especially where relationships with parents have been troubled in the past. "How can I honor my parents, when they're so whining and demanding?"

Your body is changing and you must work hard to keep yourself in good physical condition. And you're also beginning to notice

MIDDLE ADULT: AGES 50-65

OVERVIEW OF THE AGE GROUP.
1. I must make crucial choices as to the direction of the rest of my life.
2. I must give these choices meaning and commitment.

RELATIONAL
1. I must adjust to marriage without children and learn to be a grandparent.
2. My church and community work take on much greater importance.
3. My work associations lessen in importance.

VOCATIONAL
1. I need to finish the job I've chosen to do.
2. I'm a master in my field, and I can be satisfied with my accomplishments.
3. I need to redirect my time and resources into new priorities.

PHYSICAL
1. My body is declining. I must exercise to keep it as fit as possible.
2. I have the time and energy to make sexuality once again important.
3. I need to monitor all physical systems to maintain optimum health.

MENTAL
1. I now pull together all of the beliefs and values I have lived by, and integrate them into my sense of who I am as a person.
2. I can become more understanding of myself and others, and more relaxed with who I am in the world.
3. I think of all that has been, sorting, ranking and assimilating each piece of my experience into a coherent picture of myself.

that friends your age are developing debilitating health problems. Some have died.

But this can also be a new beginning for you as you again realize the importance of family and friends. Most of the vocational struggles of the past are now over. You've had a chance to realize some dreams and discard others. Now it's time to settle back and once again remember what is really important in life. It is at this time that friendship for many men becomes extremely important. There are no more corporate ladders to climb, no more financial or political dragons to slay. As you catch your breath, you may look around and find that you have no friends and desperately want a few. Or you may have a few and see those friends in a new light. You realize how important they are and have been.

The Late Adult Years (Ages 65 and over)

Dan had moved through his life taking each step with characteristic ease. He had moved into a professional career after completing graduate school. He married a woman of intelligence and poise, and together they had reared three children, who had all moved off into the world successfully. Dan had been prominent in local politics and in his church, where he had served on the elder board on occasion. And now Dan was sixty-five. He had determined to retire and turn his successful accounting practice over to a younger partner.

But then the crisis struck. Dan came home. Seems simple enough. But in his retirement, Dan came home and stayed home. In the mornings, he'd arise at the same early hour as he had when he worked. But now he'd get the newspaper and start to read. When his wife got up, he'd trail her into the kitchen and watch her fix breakfast. After that, he'd follow her around the house as she did her chores, asking dozens of questions about what she was doing. His wife was starting to come "unglued."

Now Dan sat in my office with his wife. "My only preparation for retirement had been to dream of doing nothing. I didn't realize that retirement takes strict planning and execution. I thought all I had to do was just retire. The rest would just take care of itself. Now I know I should have planned my retirement the way I planned back when I worked."

After Dan finished speaking, it was his wife's turn. "Dan's become a weight around my neck. He's simply driving me crazy." Her face displayed a mixture of anguish and anger.

It took some time before I was able to help this older couple establish schedules and guidelines for retirement. Fortunately, Dan was motivated and able to make adjustments in his daily schedule so that he could do meaningful activities away from the house, leaving his wife in peace to do her work.

The later part of life is a stage of development just as all of the others have been. It has particular distinctives and tasks that must be mastered (see summary chart on next page). If you are in this period of life, you will recognize a number of these characteristics. Furthermore, you probably will be looking back over your life and coming to terms with the way you've lived your life, the choices you've made, the things you've done and not done. Significantly, you will be considering your relationships. You may regret that you have not spent enough time with friends and family. But you may also find that you are having deeper relationships with your family now.

In chapter 7 Chaplain Halverson calls this time of life one of his most delightful experiences. "I've now discovered that my wife and my children have become my dearest friends." Unfortunately, this comment actually is in stark contrast to Dan's story. Some men do not use this time to deepen their friendships. Recognizing that their job, once a sense of identity and relational fulfillment, is gone and that their daily routine, once a source of security, is missing, they become uncertain and fearful. But this can be a period of growth and maturing. Even illness and weakness can help people to mature.

The intrusion of illness, incapacity, and finally death can cause us to reconsider what is really important in our lives. Life is fragile. One researcher into friendships, Letty Pogrebin, wrote that people over seventy years of age are the least lonely people around.[1] Pogrebin notes that people at this age have given up frantic activity and have just learned how to be with each other and draw pleasure from that experience alone.

Men, however, still tend to be lonelier than women at this age. Friendships for men have been tied to activities, work in particular. Now that work no longer offers an arena for friendships,

LATE ADULT: AGES 65+

OVERVIEW OF THE AGE GROUP.
1. I must accept my life for what it has been and the way I have lived it.
2. I must make preparations for my decline and eventual death.

RELATIONAL
1. I must learn to be in a new relationship with my wife where I'm home most of the time. I must prepare for her death.
2. My friends and church are very important, but I am also loosing my friends to death.
3. I no longer have work associates.

VOCATIONAL
1. I must find new channels for my talents and abilities for my sense of fulfillment.
2. I'm retired, and the worry of finding my way through the occupational maze is finally ended.
3. I must be careful to manage time and money effectively, realizing I might end up with too much unstructured time, and too little financial resources.

PHYSICAL
1. I continue to decline, and this worries me. How long will I be able to care for myself?
2. Sex is still an important part of my life.
3. I must closely monitor my health.

MENTAL
1. I am satisfied with my life and what I have accomplished, *OR* I live in despair for what could have been.
2. Acceptance or despair.
3. I review my life, but also attend to possibilities that present themselves now.

some men find that they do not have the relationships they once did. Men have difficulty at this age striking up friendships without the intervening activity to give the reason to be together.

When men have few or no friends, they tend to fall back on their wives or children to give the relational nourishment they need. This was the problem for Dan. He had few friends, so retirement meant that he would spend much more time with his wife.

Here is a man [King David] who has been strong and vital all of his life. Others now must care for him to keep him warm.

The book of 1 Kings offers for us, in the first few verses, a picture of David as he reaches this age. "When King David was old and well advanced in years, he could not keep warm even when they put covers over him." Here is a man who has been strong and vital all of his life. Others now must care for him to keep him warm.

And just when David is ready to turn his kingdom over to Solomon in an orderly fashion, another son, Adonijah, asserts himself and attempts to seize the throne, much the way Absalom did years before. David is just not able to retire in peace and finish off the rest of his days without struggle. But it is also encouraging to read the charge David gives to his son Solomon as he turns over his throne to him:

> So be strong, show yourself a man, and observe what the Lord your God requires: Walk in his ways, and keep his decrees and commands, his laws and requirements, as written in the Law of Moses, so that you may prosper in all you do and wherever you go, and that the Lord may keep his promise to me: "If your descendants watch how they live, and if they walk faithfully before me with all their heart and soul, you will never fail to have a man on the throne of Israel." (1 Kings 2:2–4)

In his final golden years, David still cares for others. And his relationship with his son matters much. Above all else he wants his son to follow in the ways of his God. David is still a man after God's heart.

All five stages, from novice to late adult, will challenge our ability to develop and maintain friendships. But because those stages are times of change and uncertainty, friends are worth having. And, as we shall see in the next chapter, friends can help us over the years in the most important area of all, our spiritual development.

TAKE ACTION

1. Take out your journal or a piece of paper and answer these questions:
   a. For each development stage that you have already completed, was the author's assessment valid? If not, in what areas was it incorrect?
   b. Which areas of your life get more attention—relational, vocational, physical, or mental? Look at the four areas on the tapestry of life chart (pages 110–11) and try to notice how your attention and energies may have changed over the years.
   c. Which areas in your life receive the least attention?
   d. How do you feel about your potential for growth in the later years? Do you fear these final two seasons of life or anticipate them?

2. In the previous two chapters we have looked at the challenges of each season of life a man faces if he lives a full life. Consider the stage you are in now. Generate a series of goals to begin to put more attention into areas that are now neglected. Put that list on a sheet of paper or in your journal.

10

SPIRITUALITY: FRIENDSHIP WITH GOD AND WITH PEOPLE

I was afraid. I'd never done this before, joining a group of four other men who had committed to meet together. They began meeting more than a year ago, gathering in the office of one of them each Wednesday morning at 6:30. They'd talk about the news of the day, then they'd pull out the Bible or a book that they'd agreed to be reading. They'd spend about forty-five minutes discussing the book and how it was relevant to them. Now I joined them.

The most interesting—and threatening—part would be at the end, when we would take turns talking in a circle, each man telling personally what was happening in his life, what needed prayer, and what he needed to be held accountable for that week. Lee, a corporate executive and a no-nonsense kind of person, would reach back and pull out a notebook where he kept all of the group's proceedings.

He'd look at each of us and say, "OK, Jim, you said you needed to spend more time with your son. And you agreed to take him out to breakfast this past week. Did you?"

This went on week after week for three years. To varying degrees, we opened ourselves up to one another. We went on overnights together twice a year so that we could have more time together. But more than anything else, we attempted to intentionally be involved in each other's spiritual development.

I learned to respect, even look forward to, those meetings. During the three years we met, I never made a major decision that I did not first discuss with my men's group. I had thought of moving back to Virginia the year before I actually did. I asked if the group could set aside a whole session just to discuss the 'ins' and 'outs' of that decision. Because of our discussion and prayer, I eventually concluded that the moment had not yet come for me to move. Other men in the group discussed personal struggles in their lives. Some involved marital and family difficulties. Others were having trouble with work situations and decisions. Each man brought his struggles. Each man brought his own unique understandings and perspectives to the group. Some were more willing to share and be open than others.

Horizontal relationships affect vertical relationships, and vice versa. If we have difficulties forming and maintaining earthly friendships, we probably will have difficulty forming and maintaining our friendship with God.

I've now moved back to Virginia and reestablished a private practice in counseling. I've left behind those men in my small group. But recently Lee called me to say he would be at the airport in a few hours, flying into Washington on business. He wanted to meet and chat. The timing was perfect. I swung by Dulles Airport and picked him up. We headed down the freeway and over the Key Bridge into the Georgetown section of Washington. After I'd parked and we'd found a restaurant, we both settled down into a conversation.

It was good to be back with Lee, to be catching up on a year away from one another. As Dr. Halverson has emphasized, just to be with a friend is good, and I enjoyed talking once more with Lee, the man who had hauled out his book week after week to confront me with what I had promised to do. I realized that this man, and the other men in the group, had been linked to each other in ways that none of us will ever fully understand. I have had very little contact with the other men in the group. And yet there is still a bond that holds us together.

The drama we play out here on earth has implications for the celestial drama. Part of that drama is friendships. As James Houston said, "There is a close connection between our need for richer human relationships and our need for intimacy with God."[1] Horizontal relationships affect vertical relationships, and vice versa. If we have difficulties forming and maintaining earthly friendships, we probably will have difficulty forming and maintaining our friendship with God. Therefore, as we speak of spiritual matters, let's consider the need for and impact of the "secular" matter of friendships.

When we consider forming and maintaining friendships in our lives, we are actually standing on holy ground. John sums this up in his first epistle. "We love because he first loved us. If anyone says, 'I love God,' yet hates his brother, he is a liar. For anyone who does not love his brother, whom he has seen, cannot love God, whom he has not seen. And he has given us this command: Whoever loves God must also love his brother" (1 John 4:19–21).

OUR UNDERSTANDING OF SPIRITUALITY

In many ways our minds and the way we think about things limit our understanding. When trying to understand spirituality, our individualistic American minds get in our way of understanding all God is trying to tell us. Spirituality is not an individual matter. To be really spiritual, we do not cut off all ties to other people, sell all we have, and move to a cave in the desert. That may sound very spiritual to some, but it is not a biblical model.[2]

First, a disclosure: writing this chapter caused me the greatest personal stress of all the chapters I wrote; the chapter was the most difficult to articulate clearly. This was true for a couple of reasons: (1) I don't consider myself an expert on spirituality and I struggle with the growth of it in my own life; (2) there are tricky theological implications to these concepts, and I'm not sure that I've "dotted my i's" just as I should have. As an example, the Holy Spirit is central to spiritual growth. However, I've combined aspects of His ministry with the overall relationship we have with God, attempting to be practical rather than theological. Those who wish to follow up for a more thorough discussion of developing a fuller *agape* love and our spiritual dimension through friendship can review the books listed in "For Further Reading" at the end of the chapter. I encourage you to read one of these titles.

I am especially indebted to theologian and author Lawrence Richards, who wrestled with the question, "What is biblical spirituality?"[3] I have used much of his work as a model. He found that the question was not easy to answer. But after looking at the various biblical words and considering historical theologies, Richards decided on a definition that seemed to best capture the concept in practical terms: "Christian spirituality is living a human life in this world in union with God."[4]

We can view spirituality as friendship with God. As we do so, these two themes—God is holy and God is personal—must . . . exist in a dynamic tension. If not, there is the danger that we will remake God into a celestial buddy who pals around with us, or we will be so intimidated by His awesome power that we will never draw close.

Probably the most important lesson I have had to learn is that, in many ways, spirituality is so earthy and mundane, so very unspectacular. Our model is Jesus Himself, of course—living among people, being with them, laughing and crying with them, partying with them, helping them out of jams, seeing to their needs. But in everything He did, He had perfect unity with the Father. Our unity with God does not involve a merging with Him, as some Eastern religions would instruct. But it does entail an ever-deepening relationship to Him, a relationship that has all the earmarks of a close friendship.

As we consider a direction to approach spirituality, two great themes remain foundational to our understanding of God: He is *holy*, infinite, removed, and a gulf is fixed between Himself and His creatures (this is called transcendence); and He is *per-*

sonal, knowable, and we His creatures can experience Him in intimate ways (this is called immanence). These two themes come together in the grace of God, where the holy one is brought into my heart. Once we approach spirituality from the direction that God is holy, we approach in awe, constantly realizing the great gulf between ourselves and His person. At the same time, when we approach God believing that He is personal, we come boldly to Him expecting an intimacy and a fondness to develop between us.

Thus we can view spirituality as friendship with God. As we do so, these two themes—God is holy and God is personal—must both be held in our minds, existing in a dynamic tension. If not, there is the danger that we will remake God into a celestial buddy who pals around with us, or we will be so intimidated by His awesome power that we will never draw close.

Our spirituality is forged in relationships, maintained in friendships, and will be consummated fully when we stand face to face with our ultimate Friend.

The word *friendship* doesn't sound very spiritual, but it should. Jesus has invited us to be friends, and to enter an everdeepening friendship with himself. As our friendship deepens, we grow and mature in our walk with Christ. We begin to bear fruit, demonstrating love, joy, peace, and so forth (Galatians 5:22–23). We are slowly shaped more and more into the likeness of our Friend in a process called sanctification. And, of course, we are marked more by the character of our Friend, beginning with the quality of love (which Paul goes to great lengths to explain is the true mark of spirituality in 1 Corinthians 12–14).

Our spirituality is forged in relationships, maintained in friendships, and will be consummated fully when we stand face to face with our ultimate Friend. The ultimate goal of spirituality is to be transformed. Transformation involves change, change of the very character and condition of a person. And this transformation has a lot to do with learning to live within certain relationships.

Our friendships are the building blocks of our spiritual life. Simply put, if you want to develop more deeply spiritually, first run out and find a good Christian friend and be with that friend all you can.

Spirituality involves the intermingling of the vertical dimension (placing Christ at the center of our lives, then bowing in obedience to His lordship, being absorbed in His love, and enjoying Him as personal friend), and a horizontal dimension (developing human friendships). In the vertical dimension we learn to trust and obey Christ. In the horizontal dimension our human friendships help us to shape and monitor the vertical dimension. The two dimensions always stand together, mutually nurturing each other. Our lives are transformed as we are conformed to be more like our friend Jesus Christ. The vertical and horizontal friendships will intertwine and come into play as we move through our spiritual transformation.

THE FRIENDSHIP BEGINS

Our development of spirituality begins as our friendship with God begins. God steps into the chaos of our lives and calls forth a new creation. James Houston, lecturing a decade ago, likened this recreation of our chaotic lives to the upheaval found in Genesis 1.[5] For Houston, every conversion points to the Genesis 1 account; in the midst of chaos, God steps in and calls forth order.

At a moment in time, the chaos is broken, the darkness is lifted by the light, and the structure of our lives is radically altered. All of this in a twinkling as your friendship with God dawns.

We can describe this event from many perspectives: *legally*, you're justified, *generationally*, you're reborn; from a *familial* perspective, you're adopted into God's family; in a *fraternal* aspect, you're reconciled. Each perspective points to a somewhat different understanding of this transformation that is taking place, and a different understanding of the shift in relationships that has transpired.

Let's look more specifically at these four aspects of your relationship with God. Legally, you are free, no longer bound by the cords of sin and rebellion that have held you enslaved. Once you have received Christ as your personal Savior and Redeemer from sin, you are reborn. Generationally, you find yourself in the process of being remade into the image of Christ. This involves a reorientation where you are no longer self-centered, but Christ-centered. You are becoming much more realistic about who you are. As a new person (1 Corinthians 5:17), you have a new appetite for the things of God. Motives, attitudes, values, and ideals change as you are newly energized by the power of the Holy Spirit. And, you learn to love your neighbor.

In terms of a family perspective, you become a child of God (John 1:12). Christ is your brother, and others who follow Christ are part of a new spiritual family. The entire family of believers will be reunited one day in heaven. For now, whenever you meet Christians, whether in another city or country, you are meeting other members of the family.

Fraternally, you are reconciled to God; a relationship once fractured by sin has been restored, and you draw back to God. Now you're His friend. But there is also reconciliation emerging in your relationships with everyone around you. If you're married, you treat your wife and children differently. You look on work colleagues and other associates in a whole new light. And you are able to establish new friendships that will in time begin to energize your walk with your ultimate Friend.

THE FRIENDSHIP CONTINUES

As we come into friendship with God we are transformed, and this transformation continues as our friendship deepens. Earlier in this book we talked about second-order change that radically reorders the rules of our lives (as opposed to first-order change that involves the changing of behaviors). Our experience of life is changing, beginning with our perspectives, attitudes, and values, moving into our thought processes, which in turn influence our behaviors and habits. Being precedes doing. My character is altered, therefore I act differently. My friendship with God causes me to change more and more into the image of His Son.

If you've ever had a friendship with someone you greatly admired, you probably found that you began to mimic various personal behaviors that the admired friend exhibits. When I was growing up, one of the men I admired greatly for his speaking abilities was my friend (and then my youth leader) Butch. I found, as I began to do more public speaking, that I tended to use many of the speaking techniques that Butch used. The ultimate compliment you can give someone—whether it's a high school teacher or basketball superstar Michael Jordan—is to act like him. Many school kids today play basketball with their tongues hanging out, copying Jordan's playing style. They like to "be like Mike."

The transformation in our friendship with God goes far beyond a mere mimicry of behavior. For now through the Holy Spirit your Friend Jesus actually lives within you, and as you surrender to His direction, His responses more and more become your responses. Now that's a radical concept indeed. But thus far this is all on the vertical plane. And as I've said, the vertical plane of deepening friendship must work hand-in-hand with the horizontal plane. We cannot expect our transformation into the image of our Friend Jesus to progress beyond our deepening earthly friendships.

"I just want to go off and have my relationship with Jesus, all by myself." Dragging earthly friends into the equation seems cumbersome. But it is essential, for our vertical and horizontal friendships nurture and support each other.

But we rebel at this concept. "I just want to go off and have my relationship with Jesus, all by myself." Dragging earthly friends into the equation seems cumbersome. But it is essential, for our vertical and horizontal friendships nurture and support each other. Recall Doug Coe's words in chapter 7 describing his friendship with Dick Halverson: "Our common purpose was to *help each other* achieve the First Commandment, to love God with our whole heart and then to love our neighbor as ourselves. . . . To the degree we trust God *and* trust each other, God has done great things in our lives."

MARKS OF OUR HUMANITY

In *A Practical Theology of Spirituality*, Lawrence Richards describes seven elements of our humanity, and he notes how our developing spirituality transforms each of these areas of our humanity.⁶ Each area has a personal aspect—I stand before my Friend alone (the vertical dimension)—and a corporate aspect—I stand before my Friend with my friends—(the horizontal dimension). It must be kept in mind that the corporate and personal aspects will always either enhance or distort each other. We will look at three of those marks of our humanity in this chapter, as we begin to see how friendship with people influences our spirituality—and how friendship with God influences our friendship with man.

Mark #1: I Know Who I Am

My identity requires the ability to judge who I am. This requires a relationship, because I need someone who can judge my person. I will internalize his judgments, and they will become part of my identity. Put another way, we identify who we are according to the way others identify us. Identity cannot exist in a vacuum. It emerges as we relate to others and absorb their judgments of us.

For those of us who know Christ, identity is rooted in Genesis 1, as God makes the man and declares that the creature is made in His likeness. His judgment is the supreme judgment of who we are, because He is the creator. His judgment that we are created in His image should bolster our identity as distinct people of worth.

However, because we became alienated from God, our sense of identity has been greatly distorted. With sin and a loss of His communion and forgetting His assessment of our identity, we turned to other, lesser judges to declare our identity. And those judgments, by parents, teachers, and friends, rang hollow because those individuals did not create us and were inadequate to make the final pronouncement.

Once we enter into friendship with God, however, we become aware of our true identity. *Made in His image. More than that, I now am His friend.* Those two truths—*I have His image, I have His friendship*—now fill the void of our identity.

Most who know Christ would readily acknowledge those truths. Still, many Christians question their own identity. We feel confusion about our identity, and many who embrace Christ as Friend feel inadequate and inferior. Here horizontal friendships with people can help us in the vertical friendship with God that establishes our identity. For it is at these points of confusion that our friends can surround and point us to that identity in Christ.

Consider John, a middle-aged corporate executive who came to my office suffering from an ill-defined depression. He had been a committed Christian most of his life, but the spiritual area of his life, like every other area, lacked real zest. As we talked, I soon realized John had a very poorly focused definition of himself as a person.

When John was young, his father spent little time with him. He never attended events in which John participated and excelled. John worked hard for the high grades he earned, but his father said nothing. When John was admitted to a well-known ivy league school, his father barely shrugged his shoulders. Later John married the "right" woman and had "perfect" children. He rose quickly to the top ranks of his corporation. But the harder he tried, the more impressive his résumé became, the more empty his inner life seemed to be. John was the only one who looked at his life, and he declared it to be substandard and inadequate.

John knew the right answers, that he was made in God's image, that he was God's child, that he was loved and made significant by virtue of his position in God's family. But why did he then continue to struggle with his sense of self? And more importantly, how could he now find rest in his sense of who he was as a person?

It's easy to "diagnose" John's struggles. His father never gave him a firm sense of identity. He then set out on a lifelong quest to get this sense of identity, but no one could step into his father's shoes and declare his identity. Even the Lord Jesus living in his life didn't give him the sense of identity he needed, because the vertical reality (you are in God's image and in His family) was not supplemented adequately by a horizontal reality. John had an added difficulty. He tended to project onto God the Father the images of his own father, thus experiencing God as distant and disapproving.

John did not nurture close Christian friendships; he was too busy pursuing his career path. Whenever his pastor preached on his position in Christ, John could affirm that reality intellectually, but he continued to have a feeling that God was distant and disapproving, and he had no close friendships that would underscore the reality he needed to experience day by day—that of close friends knowing him intimately and approving of him as a worthwhile person.

John's life stands in stark contrast to the lives of Doug Coe and Dick Halverson, both of whom were able to draw from each other to enhance their own personal walks with Christ. Doug and Dick both acknowledged personal inadequacies that stood in the way of developing more fully in their spiritual lives. But both leaned on the other to draw out what Christ was already doing in his life.

"John, I believe it will help you to find a small men's Bible study or support group as a starting point." We took a long look at his weekly calendar, analyzing the way he spent his time. Then we began generating goals for John, goals that included time to develop close friendships. "You really cannot fully realize your identity in Christ until you can embrace a close Christian friend who will nurture your sense of identity," I said. He agreed, left my office, and began to act on his goals. Today he is realizing more and more his goal of becoming a man who knows God.

Knowing who I am points in two directions: vertically and then horizontally. I stand with God as my Friend alone and I stand with God as my Friend with my earthly friends.[7] As I stand before God with my friends, I am accountable for the well-being of my friends and the influence I exert on their lives as their friend.

In other words, you are accountable to your friends for their sense of identity, and vice versa. Take seriously the needs of your friends because they are your friends. Confront them when they stray from the path that affirms their identity in God's image. And love them, because they are your friends.

Effective accountability often is difficult. It occurs only to the extent the confessor is willing to speak the whole truth and to accept the whole truth when it is offered by a friend. But some deliberately withhold the truth. Their lives become lies to even the closest people around them. Consequently, any effective influence on their lives from close friends is thwarted.

Sometimes we don't recognize the truth, and we unknowingly lie about who we are. We need a friend to come close and tell us the truth. Once we hear the truth, we must accept it from our friend, who will now hold us accountable.

Your friendships establish and maintain who you are as an individual. Because you have an ultimate Friend, and you have friends here on earth, you know who you are.

Mark #2: I Draw Close

We also have the need for intimacy, for drawing close and becoming increasingly familiar with someone. Richards points out that intimacy for the Christian is rooted in the man's earliest fellowship with God (Genesis 2).[8] When God created the man and woman, He placed them in the garden where He then came to walk with them and commune with them. The world was innocent, and the man could draw close to his God without fear of rejection or condemnation. He was also "naked and . . . felt no shame" with his wife (the first earthly marriage and friendship), as Genesis 2:25 explains. Intimacy with God was mirrored in intimacy between the man and the woman.

Of course, sin destroyed the vertical intimacy these two people found in their friendship with God. Simultaneously, their friendship and intimacy with each other was grossly distorted as God's friendship came tumbling down. They grabbed leaves to hide their shame from each other. They then took cover in the forest to hide themselves from God who had only recently walked with them in intimate fellowship.

At times, all of us have found our prayers becoming rigid and formal, far from the personal, intimate conversations each of us who know Christ long to have with our Friend. Why is prayer so impersonal, when we know Christ personally?

The intimacy of the friendship Adam and Eve had enjoyed with God was now broken. But God also made them a wonderful promise. This friendship could be restored as these people, and their offspring down through the generations following them, reached out to God to seek reconciliation. As friendship with God is now restored for us, we are again placed in a position of intimate friendship with Him.

This intimacy with God has a personal aspect, which involves our communication with Him through prayer, meditation, and the study of His Word. At times, however, all of us have found our prayers becoming rigid and formal, far from the personal, intimate conversations each of us who know Christ long to have with our Friend. Why is prayer so impersonal, when we know Christ personally? Lecturer James Houston offers an interesting answer: "I believe this reflects our general fear of intimacy, our fear of self-exposure, which in turn is responsible for our lack of deep friendships and, indeed, for undernourishment of our whole relational life, as we live to "perform" rather than to "be."[9] Prayerlessness is godlessness. Prayerfulness and close spiritual friendship go hand in hand, because good communication is central to any strong friendship.

According to Richards "the prayer of the heart," as exemplified in many psalms, can lead us into the deeper, more intimate conversations that God offers to us.[10] Richard Foster, in *Celebration of Discipline*, shows how believers down through the centuries have drawn close to their Friend in intimate conversation.[11] Foster says that prayer is the central channel God uses to transform us. In real prayer, "we begin to think God's thoughts after Him: to desire the things He desires, to love the things He loves."[12]

But again, this friendship with our Friend is not only a private matter. Intimacy with God is fostered as we come together as friends to worship our common Friend and encourage each other in our friendship with our Friend. God initiates the whole thing. He reveals himself to us as our Friend. We break out in praise to our Friend. And this is done with our earthly friends who encourage and enhance our experience of worship. The processes that are taking place are largely unconscious, but mutually enhancing.

Being close and intimate with my earthly friends enhances my intimacy with God. Drawing close to God enhances my closeness to my earthly friends. In fact, this is the nature of true fellowship. The community of friends gathers together to worship their mutual Friend, and in so doing, we are bound more closely to one another in love and service.

Mark #3: I Rebel, I Am Restored

The range of conflict between friends runs from simple disagreement to open rebellion. Rebellion is rooted in our sinful nature, as shown in the earliest rebellion by Adam and Eve against the standards of God (Genesis 3). In direct violation of God's mandates they decided to do things their own way. Alienation from their Friend and spiritual death soon followed.

Today, those who genuinely enter God's presence are overwhelmed with their sense of sinfulness. The light exposes the defects. When we realize that we have gone against God, there is inner turmoil and anguish. There is only one solution to the dilemma that we now face: we acknowledge that we are in rebellion, thus agreeing with God about what we have done. This is called confession.

When we initially confess our sins, we at this point become a friend of God, because the wall of animosity that kept us apart is immediately removed as God forgives us and removes the stain of sin from our lives. Now He is our Friend, but we can still do things that displease Him. And at these times we must also again confess. When we do, He forgives, and the friendship is restored to a strong footing.

Just as we offend our heavenly Friend and do those things that displease him, we also hurt and displease our earthly friends, and they do the same to us. As God our heavenly Friend forgives us, so we are to turn around and forgive our earthly friends. The two gestures obviously go together. These are two sides of the same coin: I receive forgiveness, I give forgiveness.[13]

Jesus brought this factor home in a very pointed way when he told the parable about the man called before the king to square his debts (Matthew 18:21–35). The man owed the king a fortune that he had no hope of paying. The man pleaded for mercy, and the king forgave him all his debts. But then the man, as he was leaving the king's chambers, stumbled on a fellow who owed him a few dollars. He thrashed him and insisted on his money. When the king heard of the episode, he exploded and in turn insisted that the man pay him what he owed. Then Jesus summed up the matter by saying, "This is how my heavenly Father will treat each of you unless you forgive your brother from your heart" (verse 35).

It is inconceivable that we could be forgiven by our Friend (who releases us from the penalty of our sin) and then turn around and refuse to forgive our earthly friend. But sadly, this spirit of unforgiveness is epidemic in the Christian community. What does this unforgiveness do? It holds the unforgiven friend in bondage to us. It places us in a place of judgment over our friends, instead of releasing them to relate to us in a new freedom.

Instead, as people reconciled to God who has become our Friend, we are to be "new creations," involved in a "ministry of reconciliation" (2 Corinthians 5:17–18). We proclaim to the world the message that God wants to reconcile each one of them to Himself and be their Friend (vertical). We demonstrate by our gracious lives that we no longer hold onto the failures and shortcomings people commit against us, even when these cause us pain (horizontal). We are a community of friends who freely forgive because we have been freely forgiven.

On occasion, it is difficult to tell if a sin—a willful act of rebellion against God's standard—has been committed.[14] We may have been hurt badly by a friend, but it may be unclear as to whether sin was involved. At such times, Richards states that forbearance is the route to go—viewing the person with compassion, we remain humble, patient, and gentle.[15]

But not every sin can or should be borne with forbearance. Some must be confronted, or we end up colluding in the sinful activity, and allowing unbearable pressure to be placed on the friendship. A stern rebuke at these times is called for, but again, done in the context of kindness, with a view toward healing and restoration of the relationship. To complete the transaction, the friend who wronged us should confess his wrongdoing.

David Augsburger gives a very telling example for those of us who wrestle with a friend's behavior and its effects on us. Two friends had mortgaged their homes to come up with enough cash to open up a pharmacy. One of the men, we'll call him Frank, after nearly a year of partnership came to realize that the other was embezzling cash. Instead of ringing up certain sales, the friend would enter "no sale" and pocket the difference.[16] Both were Christians.

In succession, Frank considered revenge, abandoning the partnership and the friendship, ignoring the situation to protect the friendship, and compromising his beliefs. Eventually, however, Frank decided the true biblical approach was to confront his friend in a caring way. These two actions had to go hand-in-hand if there was to be any hope of reconciliation. He had to confront the wrong behavior, and confront it in all of its wrongfulness. But in confronting his friend, he also had to express care. This was not done to gloss over the wrong being committed, but to express his ultimate love for his friend, and his hope that in confronting him, the friendship would be maintained and strengthened.

I charted Augsburger's main points[17] to look like this:

Caring	Confronting
I care about our relationship.	I feel deeply about the issue at stake.
I want to hear your view.	I want to clearly express mine.
I want to respect your insights.	I want respect for mine.
I trust you to be able to handle my honest feelings.	I want you to trust me with yours.
I promise to stay with the discussion until we've reached an understanding.	I want you to keep working with me until we've reached an understanding.
I will not trick, pressure, manipulate, or distort the differences.	I want your unpressured, clear, honest view of our differences.
I give you my loving, honest respect.	I want your caring-confronting response.

Forgiveness swirls around all of our friendships. It is a powerful weeder and fertilizer, able to pull out the destructive elements that breed between friends, while deepening the roots that bind us together.

The three marks of our humanity—identity, intimacy, and rebellion—mean we have struggles in our relationships both with God and people. But that is all part of the path to spirituality. Also awaiting along the path are issues of authority and integrity. They are among four other marks of our humanity, which we will explore in the next chapter.

TAKE ACTION

1. How have you understood spirituality and the way you've expected it to develop in your life?

2. Make a time line of your spiritual development. Begin it when you first became a Christian. Mark important periods, such as attending retreats, reading key books, and having encounters with individuals. Who was present at the important times in your spiritual journey? How did these people contribute to your development?

FOR FURTHER READING

Houston, James. *The Transforming Friendship: A Guide to Prayer.* Batavia, Ill.: Lion, 1989.

Lewis, C. S. *The Four Loves.* New York: Harcourt, Brace, Jovanovich, 1960.

Lovelace, Richard F. *Renewal As a Way of Life.* Downers Grove, Ill.: InterVarsity, 1985.

Packer, J.I. *Knowing God.* Downers Grove, Ill.: InterVarsity, 1973.

Powell, John. *Why Am I Afraid to Tell You Who I Am?* Rev. ed. Allen, Tex.: Argus/Tabor, 1990.

Richards, Lawrence. *A Practical Theology of Spirituality.* Grand Rapids: Zondervan, 1987.

Smedes, Lewis. *Love Within Limits.* Grand Rapids: Eerdmans, 1978.

11

AUTHORITY, INTEGRITY, AND OTHER MARKS OF A SPIRITUAL RELATIONSHIP

As noted in the previous chapter, in many ways our spirituality is earthy, mundane, and wholly unspectacular. Our spirituality involves time with God, and it involves time with people. And as humans made in the image of God yet defiled by sin (caused by our own rebellion), our spirituality also involves dealing with key elements of our humanity. Let's look at four more marks of our humanity and how they can be used to develop a spiritual relationship.

More Marks of Our Humanity

Mark #4: I Follow, I Lead

The exercise of authority is an important theme in the unfolding human drama. Authority has to do with the *right* to influence or direct an action. Power is the *ability* to influence or direct. For the Christian, *power* and *authority* are summed up in one word, *Lord*. In the Old Testament *Lord* was the English rendering of *Yahweh*, the God who is always present, who is not limited in time, who acts in and through us. In the New Testament the word is used for Jesus' affirming His deity and thus His authority over every natural and supernatural power.[1]

In His capacity as Lord, our Friend Jesus not only superintends the unfolding of history, He also oversees the lives of us, His friends.[2] Amazingly, our Friend is also the Lord of the universe. This is a truth we must grapple with—that the Lord of the universe is our personal Friend—much as people who are friends with the president of the United States must grapple. In many ways, the problem is ours solely, for we tend to feel inadequate. *How can the ultimate authority be my friend?* we wonder. Jesus' answer is simple and direct, "You are my friends."

As with the other issues, Jesus' lordship has personal and corporate implications. Let's look at the personal implications first. In my relationship with my Friend, I am increasingly aware that He is active in my life. I expect His interventions in my life. I also expect Him to lead my life toward what is ultimately beneficial and away from what is harmful. In my personal relationship with my Friend, I must hear what He is saying, and I must respond in obedience—communication plus action. I may hear what He says, but not take action. I may be ready to take action, but not hear.[3]

How does Christ our Friend speak to us? Though He may speak directly, often His statements come in more routine ways: the pages of Scripture, where God has spoken authoritatively, and the confirmation of friends. When we sense Jesus speaking to us, we should confirm it with those two sources. Remember too that our Friend can speak to us through an inner conviction. God can also "speak" to us while we are in prayer and meditation, bringing to mind in various ways things He wants us to know and do.

Probably the most important way that our Friend can speak to us is through our friends. This has been my experience in many different situations. I have heard the voice of my Friend through my friends who have ministered to me in countless ways.

Similarly, our Friend can speak to our friends through us. When you know a friend well, you can offer him your unique perspective and knowledge. Yet we do not want to step into roles as judges, to direct people as to what they are to do. If you move in to judge your friend's life, you move into the area of Christ's personal lordship over your friend.[4] It can be very difficult for us to realize that what might or might not be "right" for us, might be just the opposite for our friend. But it is also critical for healthy friendships that we do not move into positions as judges with friends in these areas where there are no clear biblical mandates. When we become judge, we stand *over* our friend. This is diametrically opposed to the position of friends, where each stands *beside* the other.

Mark #5: I Suffer

Adam and Eve ate of the forbidden fruit and experienced for the first time the pain of death. Though they would not die for many years in the future, death and deterioration were now a part of their world—and ours. Today in every celebration is the lurking realization that tears will soon follow. Our lot as humans has been one of suffering. And yet, we can also look ahead in hope to that day when all suffering and death will for all time be ended. In our friendships on earth, we can expect pain in the lives of our friends, and we can respond to it.

"Why me?" The words echoed through my office as Bill struggled to maintain his composure. In one year's time, he had lost his mother and his job, and now his young son had been diagnosed with terminal cancer. "I've served the Lord all of my life. I've tithed to the church, been a Sunday school teacher, an elder. How come God's picking on me?"

Those questions are as old as the Bible. Job's friends posed a theory that has plagued those who follow Christ for centuries: If you love God and do right, you'll have health and wealth; if you don't do right, everything will collapse. God quickly dispelled that theory at the end of the book of Job (42:7–10). Jesus continued to dispel the "God is displeased with you" theory of suffering as He walked this earth. (See John 9:1–3 for one example.) His words confounded the Jews, who held dearly to this theory. His words also ran contrary to the Greeks, who saw suffering as chance occurrences as impersonal fate unfolded.

By Jesus' words, and then by His own example, a new perspective on suffering was being forged. Now we were shown that people suffered for a purpose, to display the work of God. Jesus experienced intense suffering when He walked this earth. In fact, He suffered when He deserved the exact opposite. But God was there in the suffering, using the suffering to bring about redemption.

Because we have seen our Friend suffer, and through that suffering bring about our redemption, we can look upon our suffering in a totally different light. God is at work in our suffering, bringing about something good—perseverance, character, and hope (Romans 5:3–4).[5] This is, of course, suffering that comes as a result of living close to our Friend, not because we haven't done what is right.

In our vertical relationship with our Friend, as we are visited with suffering, we are to welcome it, for it is working for the good in our lives. But, as Richards points out, as we see suffering in an earthly friend, we are not to treat it as good, but to treat it as evil, and to respond with compassion.[6] There is never a sense of complacency; we cannot say, "God is working out his will, so leave it alone." No, compassion moves into action to relieve the suffering.

Several years ago I was able to visit Kenya with a group of friends from my church to learn about spiritual and physical needs there. During our visit to Nairobi, we traveled to the Mathari Valley outside town where tens of thousands of people have drifted because there is no other place to go. Their houses are constructed with whatever material happens to be lying around. Water is polluted. Food is inadequate. Medicine is almost nonexistent. As my friends and I viewed this appalling scene, each of us wondered aloud how we could help in this situation. Our attention focused on a clinic that Christians had established in the midst of that suffering, and we set about making plans to help fund the place, to help relieve the suffering there.

As we look around and see our earthly friends suffering, we will reach out in compassion to bring relief however possible: a listening ear, a helping hand, and, occasionally, flowing tears.

Mark #6: I Do What Is Right

The holiness of God reveals His character. And His character shows itself in His moral perfection, His commitment to do good, and His judgment of those who turn against him.[7] Now we as His friends are in turn called on to be holy. That's a humbling call, to be sure, as we realize our own inadequacies and the awesome demands those words "be holy" seem to denote. But being holy is a lot less spectacular than that. It involves being, then doing. We exhibit our Friend's character because we seek to be like him. We do those things which are pleasing to God because we also want to please Him.

If we are to live with God as our Friend, we are to live rightly before Him, ordering our behavior to do only what is pleasing to Him. Thus, as people look at us, they will see displayed the very life of God reflected in our person. This thought is at once thrilling and terrifying. God will display His holy character through His earthly friends who have chosen to walk with Him and call Him friend.

Our holiness is essentially a morality that calls for both a separation from sin and all evil acts, and an active involvement with sinners on their own turf. I sometimes feel that this is much like being on a diet and working in a bakery. Nonetheless, God's character, shown through us, is to come into contact with what is common and profane.

This would be a somewhat easier proposition if we could separate ourselves from the world and live with only Christian friends who, like us, were focusing on what Jesus wanted for their lives. But our holiness is essentially a morality that calls for both a separation from sin and all evil acts and an active involvement with sinners on their own turf. I sometimes feel that this is much like being on a diet and working in a bakery. Nonetheless, God's character, shown through us, is to come into contact with what is common and profane. As His friends, we are God's contact people.[5]

How can we be actively involved in a world that seems to get progressively more despicable with each passing day? Again, Jesus is the prime example that we turn to. He went about doing good, and in acts of holy living He befriended the friendless, ate and drank with sinners, and touched those who were sick. All the while He maintained His standards. People were drawn to Him because He was so helpful in what He did.

Vertically, we seek to please our Friend in all that we do. Horizontally, we do good to everyone with whom we come in contact. This doing good begins with our close friends. But then it is in many ways easy to do good to people who are our friends. Most of the time we will have good returned to us from these people. It's much harder to do good to those we don't know. It's easy to isolate ourselves from them, to close our ears to their needs, to go about our business untouched by the cries for mercy and justice that can be heard around the world, both from the community of faith and from the larger community of humankind.

But as Christians living in a fallen world, we are to respect the rights of others and to have a passion for justice that follows the example of our Friend. But what are rights, and what is justice? Rights have to do with what is due us "according to some undeniable standard."[9] The "undeniable standard" is God Himself, for justice springs from His character. When we act in accordance with God's person and standards, we act justly. When we get and keep what is rightfully ours, we say that we have been treated with justice.

As friends to the ultimate Friend, we seek justice and protect the rights of our earthly friends. We then band together with those friends to work for justice in society at large.

Mark #7: I Keep My Promises

The final mark of our humanity deals with our trustworthiness. As we develop our spirituality, we will desire and be able to keep our promises. Promising has popped up throughout this book as a foundational concept to all relationships. When we promise to do something, we make a commitment. We reach into the future binding ourselves to perform certain things in certain ways. As a friend of Christ, you are first bound to your Friend, bound to what He says brings ultimate meaning and purpose to your life.[10]

As you become committed to your Friend, you become His disciple, and slowly He will begin to transform you—gradually you become more and more like your Friend. How does this commitment work practically? It is worked out day by day, hour by hour, in the decisions you make. Living involves a series of daily choices, most of which we don't even realize because they seem so mundane. These are choices to either follow our Friend and do what is pleasing to Him, or to follow the dictates of our old self and conform to the images the world presents. Our character is slowly shaped in the daily little choices we make. And as we choose to follow our Friend in thousands of little ways daily, we find that we automatically respond as He would.

The element of humanity that seems to be eroding the fastest is commitment. People are finding ways to break their promises to each other. As commitments fail, marriages fail. As marriages fail, families disintegrate. As families disintegrate, the emotional lives of individuals are thrown into jeopardy.

That is how our vertical commitment to our Friend evolves. As we turn to our horizontal friendships, we take on a posture that runs counter to what society shows us regarding friendships, the self-serving attitude that says, "Take as much as you can from your friends." Rather than with an attitude of taking, we approach our friends from a posture of giving. "I am here to serve you," we declare. Richards defines servanthood not as "doing whatever other persons *want*; it means doing whatever we can to help meet other people's *needs*."[11] In *Celebration of Discipline*, Foster notes several active elements in serving our friends.[12] In the chart "Servanthood in Action," I have summarized seven acts of service from his book. Notice that none of these acts of service is particularly spectacular in nature. The true servant in fact gravitates toward those out-of-the-way small acts of service.

In our society, the element of humanity that seems to be eroding the fastest is commitment. People are finding ways to break their promises to each other. As commitments fail, marriages fail. As marriages fail, families disintegrate. As families disintegrate, the emotional lives of individuals are thrown into jeopardy. And the very foundation of our society is undermined.

157

SERVANTHOOD IN ACTION

1. *The service of the small things.* True servants look for the small, out of the way areas to serve, not opting for the more prestigious tasks that tend to focus attention on the servant.
2. *The service of guarding others' reputations.* We speak no evil of others, but seek to guard their reputations.
3. *The service of being served.* I allow others to serve me, and I receive graciously the acts of service given to me.
4. *The service common courtesy.* We say "please" and "thank you." We are appreciative at proper times and show other acts of courtesy appropriate to the moment.
5. *The service listening.* We focus our attention on the words of other, realizing how important those words are to that person.
6. *The service of bearing the burden of others.* People suffer greatly in this life, and we can learn to help bear these sorrows without allowing them to overwhelm us and destroy us.
7. *The service of sharing the word of Life with another.* We can bear the very words of our Friend to those who need ministry.

The friend of Christ stands out as one who keep his promises, even when it hurts (Psalm 15:4).

Let's summarize Richards' seven categories of spirituality and consider how each can impact our friendships with God and people. The chart on page 159, "The Dimensions of Spirituality," shows how each mark of our humanity adds an important dimension to our spirituality.

ANATOMY OF A SPIRITUALLY TRANSFORMING FRIENDSHIP

Solid friendships bring health. We conclude with one of my favorite stories: the spiritual healing Naomi received through her friendship with Ruth. In the midst of chaotic times when the people of Israel followed idols and "everyone did what was right in his own eyes" (Judges 21:25), Naomi, her husband, and their two sons had wandered out of Israel into Moab because there was a famine, and Moab had the food. The two sons found wives in Moab, then along with their father, they died. Naomi is left with two daughters-in-law and no husband or sons.

Naomi prepares to return to Israel a broken woman (displaying the mark of humanity known as "I suffer"), and she tells her daughters-in-law to return to their own country because she has nothing now to offer them. They are young and can find new

THE DIMENSIONS OF SPIRITUALITY

THE ISSUE	WITH MY FRIEND	WITH MY FRIENDS
I know who I am.	I am responsible	I am accountable
I draw close.	I pray	I worship
I rebel, I am restored.	I confess	I forgive
I follow	I choose	I allow freedom
I suffer	I am molded	I show compassion
I do what is right	I please God	I work for justice
I keep promises	I follow	I serve

husbands. Naomi is obviously bitter at God (displaying the mark "I rebel"), because she tells these two women to go ahead and return to their own gods. In that statement, one can sense Naomi's bitter resentment at the way God has treated her.

The first daughter-in-law takes Naomi's advice and stays in Moab. But this second daughter-in-law, Ruth, does a very strange thing. She begs Naomi to let her stay with her and pledges herself to her mother-in-law. Something has occurred prior to this that we can only guess at. This pledge by Ruth does not emerge on the spur of the moment. She has obviously thought long on this matter.

Ruth is no longer a daughter-in-law. She has no obligations to Naomi. She is young and attractive, and she would find it much easier to return to her own land and culture to continue her life. But she stays with Naomi. I can only think of two related reasons. First, Naomi, up until the tragedy, had been a woman of integrity who had great appeal spiritually and personally (Mark #1: "I know who I am"). Ruth had been drawn to her and become a close friend. Ruth had now seen her friendship with Naomi as a priority in her life. Second, Naomi has introduced Ruth to the God of Israel, and this new spiritual relationship for Ruth has transformed her life (Mark #4: "I follow").

Other elements of friendship and spirituality appear in this story. Note that Ruth's friendship with Naomi has brought her into friendship with God, and she is transformed by this experience and by her friendship with Naomi. Meanwhile, Naomi's terrible loss (Mark #5: "I suffer") of husband and sons in Moab has brought her bitter disillusionment, and she teeters on the brink of spiritual burnout (Mark #3: "I rebel"). As she returns to her homeland, she tells her family and friends to call her "Mara, because the Almighty has made my life very bitter. I went away full, but the Lord has brought me back empty" (Ruth 1:20–21). The name Mara means bitter. Naomi has been transformed from a woman whose life is full to a bitter woman whose life is empty.

Ruth came to faith and was nurtured in that faith through her relationship to Naomi. But now her friend Naomi has nothing left to give spiritually. At this point, Ruth becomes proactive. She goes out into the fields to bring in the support she and Naomi will need to survive ("I do what is right"). While serving Naomi, she then enters into relationship with the one person who can ultimately bring salvation to the family, Boaz. Naomi follows with eager anticipation Ruth's deepening romantic relationship to Boaz, and helps Ruth to strategize the various appropriate moves she will need to make to bring the relationship to fruition ("I keep my promises").

As this part of the story unfolds, another transformation is taking place in Naomi. Slowly she is being transformed from despair (1:20) to happiness (4:14–15); from emptiness (1:21) to fullness (3:17); from destitution (1:11) to security and hope (4:13–17); and from a shaky faith (1:15) to a strong faith (4:14).

Here are simple people going about their quiet lives in the midst of a chaotic world. But by their actions toward God and each other, these two friends are literally helping to hold society together.

TAKE ACTION

1. Authority, suffering and sacrifice, and trustworthiness are some of the issues we must address in our humanity. As you consider forming a friendship with another person, look at the following character traits:

   truthful speech _____

   love _____

   kindness _____

   peacefulness _____

   compassion _____

   goodness _____

forgiveness ————————————————————

faithfulness ————————————————————

self-sacrifice ————————————————————

gentleness ————————————————————

patience ————————————————————

carrying another's burdens ——————————————

Write a short definition of what each of these characteristics is like, emphasizing how it can be performed by you during the week. Now rank each of the above characteristics from one to ten (ten being the highest) as to how you feel each of these are exhibited in your life.

2. Begin praying for the right person to come into your life to help you with your spiritual journey. Pray specifically about the names that come to mind in the next few weeks. If none come to mind, the timing might not be right presently. As men come to mind, write their names down on a list and begin to think about how they will combine with your personality. Does the match seem good? Rank each person (if you have more than one) as to how well you think you will get along with each person.

3. Start with the man ranked first on your list. Call him up and ask him to breakfast. Over breakfast, tell him you are interested in a spiritual accountability relationship and ask if he would be interested. If he is, set up a regular time (weekly or fortnightly) when you can be together. Agree to get together for six times, and then evaluate the relationship at that point.

4. Show your new spiritual partner your list from #1 above. Tell him the areas in your life you are working to improve. Encourage him to make a similar list. This will be the basis for your accountability.

12

WIVES AND OTHER WOMEN AS FRIENDS

V. Raymond Edman was the president of Wheaton College a generation ago. He had a favorite expression when he referred to his wife. He liked to call her "Friend-Wife." If you are married, your wife can become your friend. And if you're single, a woman can become a friend, too.

Richard Halverson, in our talk together, spoke of how his wife had become very close to him in recent years. "When I was younger I was married to the church. I was married to my work and I devoted myself, quite without realizing it, to that work. My wife was there in my life. But she was on the margins of it.

"I would come home late at night, or I would come home having been away all day missing dinner and I would excitedly tell my wife what *we* were doing. '*We* were doing this. *We* were doing that.' One day she really rocked me when she said to me, 'When you say "we," you don't mean "us."' I realized that in my efforts to make her a part of what I was doing, I was pushing her away, because she wasn't a part of anything. The *we* didn't include her.

"Now," Halverson continued, "her friendship is the most important thing in the world to me besides my friendship with Christ."

I agree. Marcy and I have now been married for twenty-four years. Through the ups and downs of the years, I can truly say that my wife is my friend, and I value Marcy's friendship above every other earthly friendship I have. Even as I am writing this chapter, my wife and I are discussing its content, and I desire her comments about the various chapter offerings.

When it comes to friendships, most men find women a "breed apart," as well they should. As noted in chapter 6, men and women communicate differently and have different expectations. With all the challenges men face in developing friendships, committing to a friendship with the opposite sex seems full of danger. Yet that is what we do when we marry. And if you are single and dating or considering a relationship with a woman, you must consider the woman as a potential friend. For if a strong, healthy relationship is to develop, she will need to be your friend.

This chapter, then, looks at how we can strengthen relationships with women. First we will look at friendships with wives; later we will discuss the challenges of relationships with other women. Single men, and with certain safeguards, married men, can develop positive friendships with other women.

"UNCONSCIOUS" FRIENDS

A close friendship between the husband and the wife should be the goal of every Christian marriage. I think the greatest difficulty to husbands and wives becoming friends is that they live out the marriage "unconsciously"—each partner reacts to the other in predictable ways without ever stepping back to analyze why he or she acts a particular way. Marriage counselor Harville Hendrix says most marriage difficulties occur as the spouses go about unconsciously reacting to each other. Typically each partner marries seeking from the other the satisfaction of unmet childhood needs, Hendrix writes. Those needs will continue to go unmet because the partners who are selected reflect many of the negative traits of parents who were unable to meet these needs in the first place.[1]

So if Bob never felt approval from his parents as he was growing up, he marries Joyce who is not very approving either. Bob proceeds to do everything he can to get Joyce's approval, all to no avail. He seeks approval by entering into all kinds of risky business deals that demand great amounts of time. Joyce feels abandoned the way she did when she was young, so she is even more prone to be disapproving of Bob. This cycle repeats and repeats.

Hendrix says we are doomed to this unconscious pursuit of our unmet needs and never being able to draw close to our spouses in true intimacy and friendship, unless we can note the cycle and expose the needs that are in many cases fraudulent. We need to be able to say "I needed this approval growing up; I don't need it like that anymore." Then we get on with a marriage we construct consciously, where we meet each other's legitimate needs in satisfying ways.[2]

WHEN COUPLES ARE FRIENDS

So what does a conscious marriage where the partners are friends look like— A marriage where each partner is intent on growing as friends? I've found eight components to be true in these marriages.

Keeping Promises

First, the husband and wife make and keep promises. Promises bind the future and create safe places, as we've seen in chapter 4. As you promise, you vow to your spouse that exits are now closed to the relationship. You're saying, "We are in this to the end."

But not only do you promise your wife not to leave the marriage, you promise not to leave her emotionally. It is true that everyone needs alone time periodically. But men often exit from their wives emotionally in subtle ways, leaving them to wonder and hurt alone. Exiting emotionally can take many forms: we men can get lost in a sport or hobby. We can stay up late reading or watching TV every night. We can bring work home from the office and immerse ourselves in it. For couples who are friends, there are no prolonged exits that erode friendships.

Mike had been married to Jane for over twenty years. He was now well along in his career and had several children. During the first few years of marriage, Mike had worked hard to be attentive to Jane. Though he was an "up and coming" young doctor, Mike made sure he and Jane had quality time together. But as the years passed and the children came, Mike spent more time with his practice and less time at home. When he was home, he was usually distracted by household chores and hobbies. Jane got very little of his time.

Finally Mike had a short affair with a nurse he knew. Jane found out and threatened to leave. As Mike and Jane detailed their distress in my office, I was blunt with Mike. "Mike, you broke your promise to Jane, to love her exclusively. Even before the affair, you were exiting your marriage, 'having an affair,' if you will, with your medical practice." Mike hung his head and agreed.

"Mike, if you want to restore your friendship with your wife, you're going to have to keep your promises to her. Of course, that will first mean being loyal to your marriage vows. But after that, you'll have to keep your promise to be with her, not to stray into other things that would rob your marriage and your friend-wife of the best."

Love has everything to do with commitment and little to do with feelings. Couples who are friends understand this, . . . they know they will experience ups and downs, that feelings will ebb and flow.

Fortunately, this story has a happy ending. Mike was able to rearrange his priorities as Jane was able to forgive him. These two were able to build a stronger marriage based on kept promises.

Leaving Your Original Family

Second, when couples are friends, both husband and wife have left their respective families. Emotional separation from families has a lot to say about personal identity. As I leave my family of origin, with their blessing, I am stating by that action that I have a reasonable sense of who I am—my strengths and weaknesses, resources and abilities—that I can take responsibility for myself and employ my resources to survive and thrive. By letting me go, my parents are also stating they have faith in me for who I am; they are endorsing my personhood.

My separateness allows me then to enter into a close bond with another person. Otherwise, I will continue to cling to parents at the same time I am attempting to bond to my wife. These two activities tend not to exist simultaneously. Two people, a man and a wife, who are both separated from their respective families, are able to find each other and forge a friendship.

As the Scripture declares, "For this reason a man will leave his father and mother and be united to his wife, and they will become one flesh" (Genesis 2:24). Your wife deserves your full attention, and the two of you make decisions together, without the involvement of your former family. Though their advice may be considered, the decision is your wife's and yours to make. As a team accountable to each other, you can become strong friends.

Knowing What Love Truly Is

Third, the husband and wife know what love is all about. If promises are the glue that holds relationships together, then love is that special ingredient in the glue. Love finds its basis in commitment (promise). Tom Skinner, evangelist and writer, tells the story of meeting a man on a plane. The man told Tom that he was flying to meet the woman he was soon to marry, and that he had never seen or spoken to her before. "How do you know you'll love her?" Tom asked innocently. "Oh, that's easy," came the reply. "I've already chosen to love her."[3]

Love has everything to do with commitment and little to do with feelings. Couples who are friends understand this, for during their friendship they know they will experience ups and downs, that feelings will ebb and flow. But they have chosen this very special friendship, and their committed love holds it together.

Roger and Pam had been married over twenty years. Pam had suffered severe manic-depression on and off during their marriage. She was hospitalized on several occasions and had even made attempts on her own life. One day Pam was in my office sobbing. She was having a particularly hard day, and I thought it appropriate to summon her husband from his downtown job where he was a corporate executive.

Roger entered my office in his three-piece suit. He went over to his wife and knelt down in front of her, placing his hands in her hands. She looked up through her tears and asked, "Why don't you divorce me? If you do, you'll have the pick of every single

167

woman in town." Pam, with her makeup running, her clothes all disheveled, her mind confused, was right. Roger's business success matched his caring heart. I waited to see what Roger would say in reply.

Roger looked up into Pam's eyes, and said, "Twenty years ago I married you. I loved you then, and I love you now. I'm not going to leave you." Roger was a man who knew what love is all about.

Knowing How to Be Close

Fourth, couples are friends when they know how to be intimate. As you feel safe (because of promises you've made), and you know who you are (your identity is secure), then you can draw close. As you draw close, you can come to know your wife better, as she is able to know you better. There's emotional intimacy, as we become aware of and share deep personal feelings. There's intellectual intimacy where we share thoughts and ideas. There's spiritual intimacy as we can share in a pilgrimage.

As we draw closer, our friendship strengthens. Martin and Susan found this in their marriage. They'd been married over ten years, but they made their marriage friendship a priority. Every Friday night, even after children were born, they set aside a date night when just the two of them would go out. They worked hard to know each other better, to understand each other's needs, longings, hopes, and dreams. Martin and Susan had an ever-deepening friendship.

Keeping Passion in Its Place

Fifth, the husband and wife know the place of passion. Passion is the physical component of the relationship. It is the most exciting dimension—and the most dangerous. The longing and craving between a man and a woman leads to physiological arousal and an intense desire to unite with that other person. Passion, unlike intimacy, develops quickly. It also needs the protection of promise.

Passion makes the marriage friendship particularly exciting. But it is not by any means a proper gauge for the health of the friendship. Charles and Yvonne thought that it was. They had enjoyed their physical relationship together during the first few years of their marriage. But children coming and job demands lessened their passionate times together. When they came to see me, they felt that their marriage was over, because much of the "spark" was now out of it.

A good relationship doesn't experience the absence of conflict; it involves the proper management of conflict.

"Passion is the icing on the cake," I explained. "It's not the cake. Certainly there are things that you can do to bring back much of the passion you once felt. But that will ebb and flow during the years you're together. Your marriage is based on the commitment you made to one another." Charles and Yvonne did work to bring back much of the passion they once enjoyed. They also understood more fully what ingredients make a good marriage.

Knowing How to Disagree

Sixth, the husband and wife know how to disagree without being disagreeable. Relationship involves conflict. A good relationship doesn't experience the absence of conflict; it involves the proper management of conflict. When couples are friends, and conflict does arise: (1) each partner is able to articulate his/her point of view; (2) the couple can negotiate until an agreement on the problem is reached; (3) the couple can negotiate alternative solutions; (4) the couple can then decide on a course of action and implement the course decided.

Tom and Frances prided themselves that after four years of marriage, they had not had one fight. Now they were in my office and afraid their relationship was ending because they had finally had a fight. I explained to them that marriage friendships will *always* involve conflict of one sort or another. If there is no conflict, invariably someone is backing down and refusing to express his or her own needs, wants, and preferences.

We worked on disagreeing without being disagreeable. These two people learned how to have conflict in a constructive way, and their friendship was strengthened as a result.

Telling Each Other What They Want

Seventh, the husband and wife constantly tell each other what they want. Unconscious, uncommunicated, unrealistic expectations are dangerous. They lurk just under the surface, weaving agendas for the spouse. It's not the things spoken that get you, it's the things that aren't spoken.

There are two types of unspoken requests. First, the requests that are known but not said. You may have been taught never to voice a want because this was selfish. Unfortunately, your wife can't know what you want until you tell her. Second, there are requests not known and not said. You don't even know yourself what you want, but unconsciously your needs exert a powerful influence on your behavior toward your wife.

The marriage partners who are friends each know what they want, can articulate these needs, knowing that the spouse will be able to hear and meet the needs that are requested. "Frank is a very difficult person to live with," Annie explained as she sat across from me in my office. "I never know what he wants. But if he doesn't get whatever he wants, he explodes. He'll come into the kitchen while I'm cooking, and just stand in the center of the room with a blank look on his face. I know he wants something, but he won't say. So I run around getting him water, or juice, or carrot sticks, or whatever, in a frantic attempt to meet the needs he has."

Many people believe that once they're married, their partners will automatically sense all of their needs and fulfill these completely. But true friendship in marriage involves needs that are clearly articulated.

The Ability to Give and Take

In chapter 4 we looked at reciprocity, a healthy balance of give and take. Sometimes one gives, and the other receives; then they switch and the giver is the receiver, the receiver the giver. Or one leads, and the other follows, and vice versa. When couples are friends, each partner participates in this give and take.

Problems develop in two ways: The giver is always the giver, the receiver always the receiver. Their roles become fixed and unchangeable. Or, neither spouse is willing to follow or receive from the other. When one makes a suggestion, the other makes a counter-suggestion. This tends to escalate into fights.

Bruce was often frustrated with Georgianne, his wife of fifteen years. She was always needy, seeking his advice, deferring to his judgments, and following his lead. At first, Bruce had been flattered that this woman was so willing to yield to his wishes. He felt powerful and always in control. But now he wanted a wife who was more of a partner than Georgianne had been. Bruce tended to see her now as a small child, and himself as her father. This relationship was now very unsatisfactory for him.

In working with this couple, I sought to have Georgianne take more initiative at home. This was very difficult for her, for her mother had taught and modeled the role of the quiet, unassuming wife. But slowly she came to see that biblical models of marriage did not include childlike behavior that never took the initiative, and as she became stronger, she was more of a friend to Bruce, and he was most grateful.

THE NEED FOR OTHER FRIENDS

In our quest for friendships, we need look no further than our wives as a place to begin. But that is only a place to begin. We must not stop here. Wives should not and cannot be our only friends.

Like other men he knew, Eric filled his life with work and activities. He awoke early, worked hard all day, and came home late. The weekends now became cluttered with work mingled with occasional family activities. Relationships involved intermittent grunts while passing people on the way to and from various projects. Eric was the typical thirty-four-year-old successful businessman.

When he came into my office complaining of depression, I asked him about friendships. "Oh, my wife, I guess, is my one true friend. I really don't need any others besides this one." True, he and his wife were very close. They completed each other's sentences. They seemed to agree on every topic. All spare time was spent doing things together with the children. As Eric explained, "If I have any time left over from work, I want to spend it with my wife."

I began to explain to Eric that he did not have enough friendships in his life, that his wife could not supply all of his need for close friendship. Eric had trouble understanding what I was talking about.

171

"Wait a minute. My wife and I are very close. We want to do everything together. Why should I go out and manufacture friendships with other people, when I don't have the time and I get all that I need from my wife?"

Now there was a question I needed to ponder for a moment. Eric had built a strong friendship with his wife. The two apparently got along enviably with each other. Why would I want to step into their seeming bliss and create waves?

I looked Eric right in the eye and said, "Eric, your wife is not enough. Having a friendship with her just doesn't fill all of the friendship bill that you need to have filled. Simple as that."

"What do you mean?" Eric challenged.

"Wives cannot fulfill many of our needs as men and persons; they cannot fulfill all of our needs for friendship. No one person can. In fact, if you place all of your friendship demands on your wife, there's a good chance that you will begin to smother the relationship."

"What do you mean?" Eric looked puzzled.

"Many people feel that an ideal husband-wife relationship is one that is so close emotionally that each can feel each other's feelings, think each other's thoughts, drive out all differences, end conflicts, in short, fulfill each other's total needs. But this actually is a picture of an emotionally overinvolved couple that has lost much of the God-created individuality of each member in the name of togetherness. Differences, whether they be emotional, mental, or physical, are there to be celebrated, not discouraged.

"We need to befriend our wives, to be with them, to value them, to enjoy them. But we also must develop deep friendships with others, because in so doing, we are able to more easily enjoy the diversity that God has created."

It took a long time before Eric was able to begin reaching out to other men in friendship, but as he did, his life began to take on a different dimension that Eric found fulfilling. His relationship with his wife, much to his surprise, also improved, for now he was able to turn to others for some of his needs and not concentrate all of his energy in her direction. She felt relief that she was not always "on the spot" to be there for him.

In their book *In Quest of the Mythical Mate*, researchers Ellyn Bader and Peter Pearson point out that the couple must master various tasks at each stage of development so that they can continue toward deeper levels of intimacy in their relationship. But even as couples reach deeper levels of intimacy, they are also more able during certain stages to reach out beyond the marriage and form solid friendships with others.[4] To consider your marriage relationship from a developmental point of view, here are their four stages (page 174—somewhat modified and renamed by me).

According to Bader and Pearson, each stage must be taken in order. Each stage is based on the stages that have gone before (which prepares the couple for the next stage), and each stage becomes more complex.[5] Furthermore, one partner in the relationship often will enter the next stage of development before the other, thus leading to disruption and confusion for the couple.

> *Your wife cannot satisfy every need; for her space and yours, be open to developing additional friendships.*

Many of you who are scanning this chart will find yourselves in the first, "stuck" stage of development with your wife. In this stage you will have little motivation to reach out to others in friendship. Once you enter the "unstuck" stage, you will find yourself open to pulling away from your wife and seeking outside friendships.

My advice is, do it. Remember, your wife cannot satisfy every need; for her space and yours, be open to developing additional friendships. Whether you "pull away" before she does, or she moves first, a certain amount of distress will appear on the part of the other spouse, wondering if the marriage itself is threatened. It is not; in fact your marriage is starting to grow and deepen as other people enter your lives as friends.

Hank and Sue had been married for eleven years and had two children before they left the stuck stage. Gradually, though, the children demanded more of Sue's time, and Hank began to feel left out of his wife's life after years of being close friends. Hank had no real outside friends or activities. With the birth of the children, Sue became distracted in child-rearing. She also was undergoing a transition for herself where outside friends were becoming more and more important (unstuck). Hank was extremely upset that Sue was no longer as close to him as in the past.

STAGES OF MARITAL DEVELOPMENT

1. Stuck Stage

This stage involves intense bonding between the husband and wife as the couple become attached to each other. There is much passion, giving and receiving, and nurture provided by both the husband and wife. There are few demands to change, and a great deal of effort to accommodate to the partner. There is an absence of conflict. However, if couples stay in this stage, there might be intense, unrelenting conflict, as the couple is too emotionally close and fights about virtually everything. Many couples erroneously believe this stage to be the ideal relationship.

2. Unstuck Stage

In this stage, each partner begins to reestablish his or her own boundaries, pursue his own interests, and continue to develop his own uniqueness as an individual. There is a shift where each partner focuses internally in defining his sense of self with independent thoughts, feelings, and needs. There is the need for each partner not to be threatened by the spouse's differences, but to learn to celebrate the uniqueness God has created in each.

3. I-ness Stage

This is a time when each partner experiences an intense time of individuality. Each partner is learning to express him or herself creatively in the world. This can be a time of marital stress also, for each person, if not careful, can find himself drifting away from the spouse. In fact, as each partner experiences his own individuality and identity, there now is a growing need to rejoin the spouse for deeper levels of intimacy. As a consequence each person will again look to the spouse for a deeper relationship.

4. We-ness Stage

Now each partner has found satisfaction in his or her own life and has firmly established his sense of individuality (my thoughts, needs, feelings). The couple can move toward one another once again, this time establishing a deep, mutually satisfying bond. Each partner is comfortable with himself as an individual. Now each can come together and not be threatened by the other's needs, thoughts, and feelings. Each can celebrate the differences in the other and draw close to the other without losing individuality. It is here that deep, mature friendship can develop for the couple.

As with Eric in the above example, I began to detail to Hank the need for outside friendships. Over the weeks Hank began to reach out to other men and activities. He became involved with the church softball team and would stay late after games to be with friends. He and Sue now entered a stage of their lives when they were more interested in their own interests and pursuits (I-Ness). Sue became a volunteer at church and found herself on a number of committees there. Hank continued developing hobbies and other interests.

Hank and Sue continued on their own paths for several years. They did spend time together, but it usually involved activities with the children. They were not hostile to each other; they merely coexisted in the same house with different interests and activities.

Then Hank and Sue entered their final transition. They both began to feel the need for more intimacy and excitement in their relationship. And they both began to talk to the other about this. By this time, Hank and Sue had established a whole wealth of outside activities and friendships. Both were heavily involved in the church. But now the two sat down and began to set goals for their marriage. They intentionally set aside times to be alone together, and to take long weekends when they could get away. Hank and Sue now entered the 'We-ness' stage of their relationship. They did not now forsake all their outside friends and activities to come back together. They didn't need to. They now were firmly established as individuals, and now they could come back together for a closer relationship.

We begin our quest for friendships with our wives. Once we become close friends, though, we cannot cling to each other as the only friends; we must reach outside our wives to other friendships. If a man stays in the stuck stage, he may soon discover that he is unable to develop fully mentally, emotionally, and spiritually into the individual God intended him to be.

OTHER WOMEN AS FRIENDS

Men and women can find friendship with each other. And yet, even as I write these words, I can feel some anxiety begin to rise. There is obviously a danger here, a danger of sexual temptation that we all recognize can ultimately bring harm and tear relationships apart. The friendships I have experienced with women have almost invariably been in the presence of their husbands, a mutual friendship. Ruth Ann, Lynn, Carol, Diane, Peggy, Sally, my cousin Joanne, and others, though cherished friends, have always been mediated by the strong relationship I shared with their husbands.

Challenges to Friendships

For many reasons, down through history, the lives of men and women have not closely intersected. Men typically have found their working environments and their leisure pursuits and hobbies in the presence of other men or alone. Women have done the same with other women. As men and women approached each other, there seemed always present a caution, a hesitancy, a confusion of motives and signals that made the encounters even more mysterious and dangerous.

Always lurking in the shadows is the danger of sexual attraction and encounter. . . . Men find it difficult to draw close to a woman, to be intimate with her, without having sexual attraction as a prominent part of that encounter.

One reason is communication. As pointed out earlier, men and women use language differently. Furthermore, the structure and direction of our relationships are different; it is as though we have come from different worlds at times. Women seek to affiliate, to draw close, to break down status barriers as relationships are established. Men are status-conscious, competitive, adversarial, and thus usually ready to give advice, to be the expert, to take the lead (with women in particular). But these "one-up" behaviors are the very behaviors that work against reciprocity, that give-and-take that is so necessary to friendship. As a result men tend to be more satisfied with their friendships with women than women are with their friendships with men. Men get nurture and support, which they appreciate, but they tend to give much less of this in return.

And, of course, always lurking in the shadows is the danger of sexual attraction and encounter. This final danger we identify as the most sinister of all. Men find it difficult to draw close to a woman, to be intimate with her, without having sexual attraction as a prominent part of that encounter. Women, in an attempt to hold onto a friendship that they have found satisfying, may be more willing to go along with a sexual encounter, even though they realize this is not the type of relationship they wanted. The tension is there, and it ebbs and flows for as long as the relationship exists.

Once sex has been introduced between a man and a woman, the relationship immediately and unalterably changes. The rules change. The expectations are all different. The man and the woman find themselves in new territory that might prove to be very frightening. Scripture mentions the mystery that surrounds sexual relations, the physical and emotional joining of two people into one. No amount of experimenting by sexual researchers can capture this mystery. Because of this, Christians realize that there is no such thing as a casual sexual encounter. Every sexual encounter is potentially life-changing.

Even if the sexual tensions can be mastered, even if the relative differences between the sexes can be somehow neutralized, there is also the issue of other people that must be considered. People generally jump to the conclusion that if a man and a woman are together there is romance between them, and a sexual encounter cannot be far off. This is true even in the Christian community.

THE REWARDS OF FRIENDSHIPS

Having looked at the dangers, we should highlight the benefits of friendships between the sexes. Of most importance is the idea of perspective. Women see the world differently than men do, and men need their perspective to gain a more well-rounded picture. Women can teach us how to affiliate and draw close in ways that are enriching and enhancing. Men over and over have told me how satisfying it has been to have a female to whom they can turn, a woman who was willing to listen uncritically. For many men, this has been the first such experience since their own mothers sat on their beds at night and listened to the recitation of that small boy's adventures from that day.

When men and women are able to forge friendships, they must recognize that they have different perceptions as to the value of the friendship and of intimacy and closeness. Men tend to be more satisfied than women about their cross-sex friendships. This is also true in marriage: husbands are more satisfied with their relationships than wives are. Why is this? Probably because men expect less from relationships generally than do women. Men are more satisfied with less depth to the relationship.

But it is also worth noting that men have again and again reported that their friendships with women provided them with the nurture and intimacy they could not find in their friendships with men. When talking with a woman friend, men are less defensive, feel less competitive, and are more understanding generally.

So the men enjoy their friendships with women. The women, however, are less excited about these relationships. Women are used to drawing close and nurturing in friendships. To them this is no big deal. If you ask a woman whether her male or her female friendships are more satisfying, she'll probably say her female friendships.[6] "In my relationships with men," one woman reported, "he talks, I listen." Reciprocity can be sadly lacking.

As men talk, they seek to preserve their independence and maintain their status. None of this disposes a man to be a particularly good listener.

Men usually discuss different things with their female friends than with their male friends. Men go to both men and women to discuss work. But if there's an intellectual problem, he'll probably turn to a man. If he wants to talk about relational difficulties, he'll probably turn to a woman friend.[7]

Women, in discussing their friendships with men, note that usually they are the listeners, while the men talk. The linguistic experts are beginning to find the same pattern. Evidently men, paying closest attention to status and hierarchical order ("Am I one-up or one-down in this relationship?"), pride themselves in dispensing information, giving advice, and being the expert (all one-up positions).

As men talk, they seek to preserve their independence and maintain their status. None of this disposes a man to be a particularly good listener. He either challenges the woman's assumptions or gets distracted and loses interest when he can't see much of a point in what is being said. When she mentions a problem, he gives a piece of advice and moves on quickly. Simply put, when problems need discussing, men look for solutions, and women look to understand the process. The woman asks, "What was he thinking and feeling when he said that?" The man, behavior-oriented, asks, "How did she react? Why?"

In general, men are leery of intimacy. To draw close, to open up and express feelings, to say what is really going on inside seems strange and threatening. But in spite of all of these differences, men and women are still drawn toward each other in friendship, realizing that each has a unique perspective on life to offer the other.

THE DEADLY TEMPTATION

But I know, even with the benefits firmly in mind, most men will weigh these against the dangers, and decide that close friendships with women just aren't worth the risks. My friend Tom Eisenman notes in his book *Temptations Men Face* the dangerous steps that a man takes as he begins to walk down the road toward an affair.[8] The steps begin with readiness and culminate with acceptance. Along the way the man participates in an emotional dance through increasing time together that heightens the man's attention to the woman. Actual physical touch does not occur until step 9, but the man has prepared himself emotionally for the moment.[9] The emotional dance between them can be beguiling and very dangerous.

Lewis Smedes describes the danger well: "When a man and a woman enter each other's lives, their separate mysteries almost immediately begin to unfold to each other. And as they begin to unveil their mysteries, they are taken into an emotional flow that will carry them to places neither has been before."[10] The bonding is very intense, drawing each to the other, and it is nicely rationalized because, "We haven't been to bed together."

Given all of this, can there be some test to measure whether my friendships with women are innocent and God-honoring, or illicit and headed for more trouble? Smedes offers a simple question every married man should ask: "How does this friendship with this woman affect the primary covenant I have with my wife?"[11] This can be difficult to determine, and this is where accountability is critical. If you are currently in a friendship with a woman, and there are aspects to the relationship that cause you or your wife to be uncomfortable, I would encourage you to seek out a trusted friend or your minister and spread the situation before him to get an outside opinion.

Friendships between men and women are possible, though there are dangers that lurk. Pogrebin lists the following four criteria for a person to be able to maintain and establish a satisfying cross-sex friendship:

1. He has lived close enough to the opposite sex to be able to experience women as "regular" people.

2. They met in a context (work or other activities) that started with each seeing the other as an equal, as opposed to a boss-employee or teacher-pupil situation.

3. At least one of the two friends does not follow strictly to sex role stereotyping (for example, men never show their feelings).

4. They don't have sex together.[12]

WHEN YOU'RE SINGLE

One can argue that it is easier to have female friends if you are single. Introducing a wife into the cross-sex friendship equation can be very difficult.

It must be remembered that many marriages begin as friendships between two singles. As their friendship deepens, feelings of love begin to intervene. In my experience, these friendships turned to marriages prove to be very strong unions because they are founded on strong friendships first.

But there are also difficulties for single men who make friends with single women. The greatest difficulty that I have seen has been in the area of expectations. Expectations surround all relationships. Most of these expectations are never spoken; many lie buried within us and are never consciously known. As single men and women form friendships, the expectations of each may run at cross purposes from time to time, each expecting different things out of the relationship. Often, one person hopes or expects the other to develop romantic feelings.

Rocky had that problem with expectations when he came to see me. He'd known Carey and had been close to her as a friend for a couple of years. He had enjoyed Carey's friendship as they had participated in many activities either alone or with a group of people. But now Rocky was in my office complaining. "Carey, I think, sees our relationship as more than just a friendship. I think she's fallen in love with me, and wants us to become sweethearts. That's not where I am at all. I want to remain friends with Carey. It's a really important relationship for me. But I don't know what to do with her feelings toward me now."

Rocky's lament has been echoed by many in my office. The expectations are out of kilter, and I set about attempting to put those back in order again. "Rocky, I think it's time that you and Carey have an honest talk about your relationship. You'll need to sit her down and tell her you sense that expectations have gotten out of line."

Rocky came in the next week and said he and Carey had discussed their expectations. She had cried and admitted that she wanted more from the relationship than he was looking for at this point. They also talked about whether it would be too painful for her to continue as friends at this point. She told him she didn't know, but she would be clear with him as time went by.

Friendships with women offer new opportunities and perspectives for men. But there are also dangers. Men handle relationships (beginning with conversations) differently than women do. Sexual tensions and allurements also lurk in the shadows and must constantly be monitored. But my friendships with women have been very rewarding, and I would encourage you to consider them as a possibility as you continue to venture into friendships.

TAKE ACTION

1. Overall, how would you characterize your relationship with your wife: Distant, somewhat close, or a close friendship? Can you see how your relationship has ebbed and flowed over the years of your marriage? Which transitions have been the most difficult for you?

Sit down with your wife and together draw up a set of goals for your relationship. You can begin by making separate lists. Then compare your lists and combine these into one list. Note that each of you will have different priorities as to what goals are more important. Take out this list each year on your wedding anniversary and update it.

2. Have you had friendships with women besides your wife in the past? What are/were those relationships like? Sit down with a female friend and answer this question together: How is the relationship with this woman similar/different from your relationships with men?

3. Have you and your wife ever sought out another couple in friendship? Sit down with your wife and consider the benefits you can remember from those couple relationships.

13

WHEN A FRIENDSHIP FADES

King David decided to flee the capital city for his very life when his son Absalom attempted to usurp the throne. With looks and charm, Absalom seemed to be succeeding in the attempt. Ironically, at the very moment David was fleeing, a man he knew well was approaching Absalom to offer his services. Ahithophel was the most trusted counselor David had. More than that, Ahithophel was David's friend.

As David fled for his life, his close friend and adviser went over to the enemy to offer him his services. Betrayal!

Later, as David sat in exile wondering whether his kingdom had truly passed out of his hands, he did what he liked to do to settle himself down. He composed a poem. In that poem, which became Psalm 41, he wrote, "Even my close friend, whom I trusted, he who shared my bread, has lifted up his heel against me" (9). David echoed his feelings of intense, deep pain in Psalm 55, where he wrote, "If an enemy were insulting me, I could endure it; if a foe were raising himself against me, I could hide from him. But it is you, a man like myself, my companion, my close friend, with whom I once enjoyed sweet fellowship as we walked with the throng at the house of God" (12–15).

Friendship can be such a fragile thing. Like any relationship, it is subject to the storms and stresses and sometimes bitter endings, as David suffered with Ahithophel. George Washington once observed, "True friendship must undergo and withstand the shocks and adversity before it is entitled to the appellation of friendship."

One set of researchers observed that a friendship endures less conflict than any other relationship that we have.[1] Could that be because we just go ahead and dissolve a friendship quite easily when conflicts arise? Or do we, once we have established a deep friendship, work harder to maintain the relationship through the storms?

This chapter has been difficult to write; it required that I recall friendships that once were but which now have dissolved. I also must look at present relationships with which I am struggling.

WE DRIFT APART

Herb Short and I had been friends since college. We both married and settled in the same area. We often got together with our wives and, when kids came along, with our families. Holidays were usually spent at least in part with the Shorts. Herb and I enjoyed an easy manner with each other, and we could complete each others' jokes and stories. We also shared many important events together and didn't need lots of explanations to catch each other "up to speed."

It's difficult to pinpoint when things started to drift between Herb and me. I don't think I can even articulate accurately what the issues were, indeed if there were any specific issues that came between us. We just seemed to call each other less. On special occasions we didn't think of the other first to invite for the celebration. Conversation became more strained. When he and his family finally moved away from the area, our friendship had pretty much terminated. There was no formal farewell to the relationship. Neither of us even spoke of it as an ending. But it truly was an ending.

REASONS WE DRIFT APART

Friendship can run into trouble for a variety of reasons. Pogrebin lists ten reasons,[2] which I have combined into six; the first four involve drifting apart, and we will look at those first. We will look at the final two reasons later in the section entitled, "We're Torn Apart," for sometimes separation from our friends can be more painful and shocking.

A Third Party

The first reason friendships run into trouble is a third party enters the scene. When both friends are single, one of the friends may fall in love and get married; the friendship may be in danger of ending. I've heard the complaint on many occasions that a woman came along and stole the heart of a friend. The whole nature of the friendship changed. No longer was the newly-married friend available on the spur of the moment. No longer could the two friends talk till all hours about whatever came to mind. A third person had now stepped between, and the friendship would never be the same.

The entrance of children into a friend's life can also be the third party that can sour the relationship. Now your friend is distracted. This time the third party, a child, can be very demanding of time and attention.

Separation and Divorce

Second, separation and divorce can destroy friendships. I've seen several of my friendships end as my friends went through a divorce. In some cases I was angry at my friend's decision to divorce. In other situations I felt loyalty to the friend's ex-spouse and was not able to offer the support the divorcing person needed. I asked myself, *Should I ignore what is happening? Should I confront my friend?* Many of these situations seemed confusing and not clear-cut. I was unsure as to who was the guilty party and whether I had a role in determining this and rectifying the situation.

During one marital breakup involving friends, I jumped squarely into the middle of the situation (uninvited by one partner) and attempted to do unsolicited counseling to save the marriage. The whole thing blew up in my face with both partners turning the anger on me. I limped away hurt and confused and watched helplessly as my friends divorced.

In any case, divorce rearranges all of a divorcing person's relationships, and friendships suffer as a result.

Competition and Envy

Third, competition and envy can damage and end a friendship. My friend has what I do not have, and I want it. It is difficult to remain friends when I've felt as though my friend had more and better of what I wanted, be it money, talent, opportunities, or people. At this point, however, we must look within our own heart to determine what is truly the most important thing.

I've had several friends who made a great deal more money than I did. As a result, they could engage in activities and own things that I could never dream of having. But I also came to cherish their friendship. I realized that many very wealthy people are also very lonely people. They are envied on the one hand, and solicited for donations constantly on the other, and it is difficult for them to have friends who aren't after them for something.

I found that I could reach out with the one thing they didn't have and the one thing they most needed—I could reach out and become their friend. I'd have a group of men over for sporting events such as the Super Bowl and just have a time of refreshments and enjoyment around the event. At first it startled me how quickly men who were far above my economic category would respond positively to the invitation. Once together, everyone enjoyed himself and there was never a sense that one had more material things than another.

Becoming Uncomfortable with a Person's Beliefs or Actions

Fourth, learning something new about the person's beliefs or actions can cause us to reassess our friendship. Once I was with a friend I'll call Jack when he displayed a sudden burst of anger; later he uttered an opinion out of the blue. In an instant I saw Jack in a new and troubling light. At that point his life was not matching his words. I realize that I have struggles in my life, also, and that friendship demands tolerance. But these breaches seemed to be denied by the person himself. I became very uncomfortable with the behavior of my friend.

Has that happened to you? In chapter 4 we mentioned that a developing friendship requires that we respect the other person's perspective. But what if the person seems to reveal fundamental character flaws, and we are not comfortable?

I would hope that true, deep friendships can survive those sudden, negative revelations that intrude into our relationships;

it was difficult for me to accept Jack. Many casual friendships cannot accept such revelations, for the time needed to explain and repair these upsets can be substantial. In contrast, true friendship has a lot to do with holding each other accountable and pointing up and helping each other through our own inconsistencies.

HOW WE DRIFT APART

Drifting apart can take several distinct forms. We may begin to distance ourselves from each other. Distancing can take place geographically, and we simply do not go to the same places where our friend is. Or it can be an emotional distancing. (Women seem to intuitively feel emotional distancing much more quickly than men do.) Little by little, our friend somehow doesn't seem to be present, even when he is in our presence. He also says less about himself and his life. Talk becomes superficial, straying to topics that have no personal content.

My friend Joe saw what I was doing as disloyal to him and to the implicit promises I had made for a private practice with him. With this charge of disloyalty, our relationship had the potential to blow apart. It almost did.

One way a friendship may drift is by one person provoking a fight. Ultimately we can end the friendship by having a strong dispute. Another way is to become annoying and difficult to be with. In either event, our behavior provokes the friend to begin to drift away.

The deeper the friendship, the more intertwined the participants' lives become. These friendships have a way of involving other people also. As these friends begin to come apart, disentangling themselves from each other's lives can be very difficult. If these friendships must end, it is best that they end out in the open and definitely so that everyone understands what has happened. Sadly, this is rarely the case. And as two friends part company, their families and other friendships often suffer.

WE'RE TORN APART

Joe, Rich, and I had been friends a long time. Rich and I had done youth work together more than twenty years ago. Joe, Rich, and I had worked in public mental health together when we were first getting our starts in the counseling field. We had laughed and cried together. We had hammered out our theories of counseling together. Eventually we decided to buy a condominium and set up a private practice together.

We were together in this practice less than a year when I got the call. A minister friend in California, senior pastor of a very large church, wanted me to come and run his counseling center. I would run the center, plus preach, teach, and have time to write, all of which I wanted to do but never had the time.

I was confused about the right decision. God seemed to be slowly opening the doors for me to go. And yet there was a major obstacle for me. My friend Joe saw what I was doing as disloyal to him and to the implicit promises I had made for a private practice with him. With this charge of disloyalty, our relationship had the potential to blow apart. It almost did. I moved to California but struggled with my relationship with Joe for five years. I knew I had hurt him, and yet I was unclear as to how to repair the relationship. Fortunately, I was able to return to Virginia, and Joe and I, with Rich's help, were able to talk through point by point what had happened, and reestablish the friendship that had meant so much to both of us.

Sometimes friends don't drift apart, they're torn apart, and the friendship ends abruptly. Lewis Smedes in his helpful book *Forgive and Forget* lists a descending order of deep pains that wound us.[3] There are many annoyances in our lives, followed by various slights we experience as snubs. Next in our pain comes disappointments, as people don't do what we expect them to do. Following this is the pain of coming in second, especially when it is your close friend who comes in first and wins the prize (of promotion or acclaim). This is a form of jealousy, born of our competition.

But Smedes explains that the pain intensifies with two final categories that seem, more than the others, to rip apart friendships: disloyalty and betrayal. His list echoes the concerns of Letty Pogrebin in her book *Among Friends.*

Disloyalty

Fifth, disloyalty wrecks friendships. "I thought I could trust him. And he turned around and knifed me in the back." Smedes says that when we act disloyally, we treat our friend as a stranger.[4] Disloyalty has to do with the breaking of the spoken or unspoken promise between the two of you.

Albert had revealed many painful things to Dave about his marriage. He'd cried and prayed with Dave, and he asked Dave to hold him accountable to work on a stronger relationship with his wife. When a man Albert hardly knew approached him after church one Sunday and asked how he was getting on with his wife, Albert felt hurt and angry. This man said that Dave had told him Albert was having troubles in that area. Albert mumbled some reply and stalked off to find Dave.

Dave was repentant, stating he had merely mentioned Albert's troubles to a few men so that they too could pray. But Albert felt the disloyalty. Albert was also very reticent to tell Dave any personal information of consequence in the future.

Betrayal

Sixth, betrayal is the most dangerous and the most hurtful reason that friendships end. Many friendships end this way, with the ultimate pain from a friend, the pain of betrayal. The friend now treats you like an enemy. Peter was disloyal to Jesus, treating him like a stranger when he denied he knew him. Judas betrayed Jesus when he sold the teacher to his enemies. And Ahithophel abandoned King David to serve David's son during a rebellion. The wounds of betrayal are the hardest to heal. We trusted. We opened our lives to this person and were vulnerable. And then the person took us and dashed us. The friendship is immediately over. Now begins the painful period of healing and forgiveness, a period that can stretch for years.

Andrew was a true friend. We got together on many occasions, enjoyed many of the same things, blended our families together for various activities. Our wives enjoyed each other also. Even our kids got along.

But then Andrew became involved in a shady deal. And a number of people, also friends of mine, were hurt as a result. Andrew's name became smeared in the community, and, sadly, most of what was said about him was true.

I found myself terribly confused. Is this a time to stand by Andrew and lend him support? *I wondered. . . . Should I . . . lovingly confront Andrew with his lies and deceit?*

And to top it off, Andrew responded poorly to the situation. Instead of acting repentant and remorseful for all the people he'd hurt, he excused himself, he played the victim, he declared how he was almost (if not entirely) innocent of any wrongdoing. Trying to talk with him became difficult. Most people abandoned him, not knowing how to deal with him in this present situation. I found myself terribly confused. *Is this a time to stand by Andrew and lend him support?* I wondered. I was nervous about this, because I knew Andrew was in extreme denial, and supporting him now might give him the strength he needed to continue in his false sense of reality. But he was also my friend, and I felt uncomfortable abandoning him also. Should I be the one then to lovingly confront Andrew with his lies and deceit? Unfortunately, I did not possess the pertinent information needed to make such a confrontation constructive.

And even though Andrew's behavior had not directly affected me, I somehow felt that he had betrayed me also. I had trusted him to be completely honest in all of his business dealings, and he had not been. I had referred people to him, and these people had been hurt.

So here I was, left with these alternatives: (1) give Andrew complete and unconditional support because he was my friend; (2) abandon Andrew and never speak to him again until he was willing to repent and come to his senses; or (3) confront Andrew with his wrongdoing, even though I was not in a position to weigh the facts fairly. As with so many people I see in counseling, I felt I was left with only bad alternatives.

I decided on a fourth course. I chose to tell Andrew that I had struggled with this matter for some time, that the whole episode had caused me a great deal of personal pain. I told him that I was not in a position to weigh all the facts, but what I had heard from a number of trustworthy sources was consistent. I told him that I felt he was in a state of extreme denial, deceiving himself as to what he had done and the harm he had caused. I told him that I forgave him for the pain he had caused me, but until such time as I became aware that he had made significant changes in his life, I would no longer associate with him.

DESTRUCTIVE RELATIONSHIPS

Certain relationships, forged at first with the expectation of being true friendships, turn out to be destructive as time passes. Such relationships also must end, for they are not healthy and can never be true friendships. We've touched on the first three of these previously. Let's look at these and two other relationships that go badly for people.

Dependent Relationships

Instead of being reciprocal, the dependent relationship finds one of the people involved becoming dependent on the other over a period of time. No longer does the energy flow back and forth between the friends. Now one is put in the position to nurture the other. Of course, this happens from time to time in any relationship. But in a destructively dependent relationship, the dependence remains in place, with one person always depending on the other.

Possessive Relationships

The possessive relationship is a cousin of the dependent relationship. In this relationship, one "friend" possesses the other and becomes jealous when the other draws others into the relationship. The first friend is thinking, *I must have you all the time. I'm not complete without you.*

I once had a friend like this. He always resented it when our twosome became a threesome. He didn't want to hear about other friendships that I was enjoying. He really didn't want to hear about activities that I had done without him. He wanted a friendship that was exclusive. I realized that I could not have a friendship on these terms, that this in fact was no friendship at all, but a very possessive relationship that made me feel smothered and uncomfortable.

The Hidden Agenda Relationships

Relationships with a hidden agenda look at first like true friendships that are beginning to sprout. But as time passes, one or the other of the people involved springs an agenda on the relationship that was not at first spoken. The goals are not just friendship.

The first time I met Max I liked him. He had a broad, easy smile and a firm handshake. He had approached me on the patio after church, introduced himself, and told me he was intentionally seeking me out because he wanted to get to know me better. I was flattered. I quickly made time for Max. I wanted to know him better. He was so friendly, so at ease, so vulnerable about himself and his family.

Max and I finally got together and sat down in a local restaurant over breakfast to chat. Max was again his smiling affable self. But as the conversation continued, I realized that Max had an agenda. "Jim, the real reason I wanted to sit down with you today was to make you aware of an exciting business proposition that you can get in on if you act fast." I felt crushed and somewhat betrayed. I thought Max really wanted to get to know me. He merely wanted to sign me up so he could make money. I didn't mind Max making money. I didn't even mind if Max solicited me in his business. But I didn't like the fact that he was not up front about his business and seemed to conceal his true intentions behind the guise of wanting me as a friend.

Co-dependent Relationships

Another unhealthy relationship that cannot grow as a friendship is the co-dependent relationship. Co-dependent relationships occur if we inadvertently enable bad behavior in another to develop or to be sustained. We collude in destructive patterns. This concept has grown out of the ranks of alcoholic families where family members have unknowingly become involved in the drinking behavior of the alcoholic, promoting it or sustaining it by what they say or do—or do not say or do. They help sustain the behavior by their presence and support, and the person with the bad behavior inadvertently depends on the other people to help him maintain his bad patterns.

Many habits and character patterns are destructive that we can knowingly or unknowingly collude in with our friends. Perhaps you have a friend who is always critical or demeaning of other people. Or you have a friend who dominates every relationship and never lets anyone else initiate the action or speak their mind. Perhaps you have a friend who drinks too much, or gambles away all of his money, or chases after women, or uses profanity. Instead of confronting him on this behavior, you merely laugh when it occurs, or you ignore it. By doing this, you encourage the friend to continue it.

Deep friendship involves being able to confront each other and hold each other accountable.

Not only do we encourage behavior that is obnoxious, inappropriate, or sinful, we also prevent the friend from making changes in this behavior. With a nonconfrontational approach, we provide a satisfying, comfortable relationship that says to our friend in effect, "Go ahead, keep on doing what you're doing. It doesn't make any difference to me. With my silence, I accept you and all your behavior. There's no need to change a thing."

Deep friendship involves being able to confront each other and hold each other accountable. I want what is best for my friend, and if I see him stray into areas that are not helpful, or are just plain destructive, I am there to point up the trouble.

Avoidant Relationships

Avoidant relationships are friendships where no issues critical to the relationship are ever dealt with. When something comes up between the friends, it is ignored, left to fester in the shadows of the relationship. Such friendships are not built on honesty and openness. As pressure builds up between the friends, and no effective communication on difficulties has ever taken place, the friendship usually blows apart.

FOR FRIENDSHIPS THAT ARE ENDING

If you have had several friendships end, or a friendship seems to be drifting, the following questions are worth asking. They can help you check motives and patterns in your friendships.

1. Think back to several friendships you've had in the past that now have ended. Did these break up dramatically, or did you drift apart?

2. Did the breakup of these friendships have something to do with how much or little you valued friendship?

3. Do you feel that you had been fair with your friends that you broke up with? Have you taken the time to consider the importance of your friends, and the reasons to dissolve the realationships?

4. Think now about a particular friend in a current relationship. Are you angry or dissapointed by what your friend *has done*, or who your friend *is*? Can you pinpoint a particular habit or behavior that your friend can change so that the friendship can survive?

5. Can you discern a pattern of friendship breakups in your life? Are there things that you need to change about yourself that may be contributing to these breakups?

Clearly, friendships end for a variety of reasons. When a friendship is ending, you may want to evaluate the reasons. The sidebar, "For Friendships That Are Ending" (above), offers a series of questions you can ask yourself when a friendship seems to be fading to black.

FORGIVENESS

We have been hurt in friendships. Many of you who are reading this book are still struggling with past betrayals by friends who have left lasting scars. The pain is very real. But what are we left with? As people who know Christ, we can turn to the one faithful Friend as an example. Remember, Jesus was betrayed by friends, yet He was also able to forgive, right up until the moment of His unjust death.

Through Christ's sacrifice I have been forgiven by God. And as I reach out to accept my own forgiveness, I now have a new perspective on my own shortcomings and failings. "Woe is me! for I am undone" (Isaiah 6:5, KJV). We fail people too. We may not be responsible for all that may have been done or not done to us by those we once called friends. But we are responsible for what we do with all the bitterness that has been engendered. I have been forgiven by God to forgive others. How could I not?

Why is forgiveness so important? Why am I called on to forgive people who have mistreated me in the past? Here are four reasons we must forgive those who hurt us:

1. Forgiveness levels the playing field. It puts you, the forgiver, on the same side as the person who did the wrong. You recognize the truth: "I'm really no different from him." When you forgive you acknowledge you're no better, really, than the person who mistreated you.
2. Forgiveness releases the past. It loosens the stranglehold of guilt on us and others. To remain bitter is to allow oneself to continue to be abused or betrayed or mistreated.
3. Forgiveness gives us a new perspective. By forgiving you begin to see the person who hurt you through God's eyes. And you can also see how God even uses the mistreatment to further His ends in your life: to mold you into the image of your Friend.
4. Forgiveness breaks the cycle of blame and pain in relationships. I've seen broken friendship where two stubborn people square off about who's right and what really happened. Neither will back down. Forgiveness in these situations doesn't solve the sticky questions of justice or fairness. Many times it sidesteps these. But it does allow relationships to start over. I realize that it may not necessarily mean a new relationship with my friend. He may not understand or even care. But the possibility is there.

AN ALTERNATIVE TO LETTING A FRIENDSHIP FADE

Unfortunately, men find it so easy to walk away from friendships. Again, we give these relationships so little value in our culture. In contrast, Dick Halverson and Doug Coe (chapter 7) would find it inconceivable that they could ever drift apart as friends. Both men emphasized over and over that they were friends for life.

As we make friendship a priority and invest more of ourselves into a relationship and truly commit to our friends, we will find it much more difficult to just drift apart. But I think another step can also be very helpful, one that Dick Halverson and Doug Coe took to cement the friendship. They began to speak openly to each other about their commitment. In effect, they covenanted to be there with each other through thick and thin for the rest of their lives.

Few formal covenanting ceremonies remain in our culture. The marriage ceremony is the most obvious and dramatic. It also contains many of the covenanting elements that have been passed down to us from ancient times. Not that we need elaborate rituals to seal our bonds. But I find that rituals are helpful for people to establish significant points in time and to clarify expectations.

In ancient times, if I intended to make a covenant with a friend, the two of us would meet on a designated day. A lamb would be split down the middle, and the two halves would then be laid apart. My friend and I would stand in the middle of the two halves and pledge our loyalty to each other. Our wrists or palms would be cut and our blood mingled together. We would exchange belts ("Your enemies are now my enemies") and rings ("Your possessions are now my possession").

Friendship rituals that we now invent won't be as elaborate as those. However, with the dearth of rituals in our society, a friendship ritual today would take on true importance. Therefore, if you have a special friend, you may find it helpful to discuss the possibility of creating a ritual to cement your friendship with each other.

TAKE ACTION

1. Review the questions in the box "For Friendships That Are Ending" (page 194). Then take out a sheet of paper or your journal and write a short account of one friendship that ended for you, one that is still vivid in your memory. Think of what you and your ex-friend did and *did not* do that contributed to the breakup. Make a list of things you could have done to have salvaged the relationship.

2. If you have a friendship that seems to be drifting, discuss openly with your friend the difficulties between you. Allow him to discuss his perspective and concerns in a true dialogue.

3. Have you had a friendship break up and you are unsure of the reasons? Plan to meet with the person. When

you meet, ask him why he thinks the friendship has dissolved; then you should indicate why you think it ended. If neither knows why, ask what he liked about the friendship and what he didn't like. By doing this, you should get to the cause of the breakup. You may not be able to restore the friendship, but you will understand your goals in friendship better, and you may know yourself better, thanks to your former friend's perspective.

14

HOW TO BEGIN

True friendships are indeed bonds of iron. They give us strength to endure setbacks, misunderstandings, and loss. They help us understand ourselves and contribute to others. And a good friend will point us to even a more abiding strength in our friendship with Christ. I trust you've been able to see the critical importance of friendship in your life and are ready now for some practical steps to either strengthen relationships you already have or start friendships that you've never had. It's time to underscore the important points and to look to ways to put these points into action in your life.

As you read through this final chapter, keep several truths in mind. First, friendship takes time. You will have to carve out times from your busy schedule to be with people. There are no shortcuts. If you want to have close friendships, you have to be with friends to develop the relationships. Second, friendships take work. Close friendships don't just happen (neither do strong marriages). Friends have to work at their relationship all the time to make it robust. Otherwise, the relationship will slide downhill and be less fulfilling to both people.

Finally, friendships are not just "discovered," they are sought after and built. This requires an active approach; you will not find close friends by walking to the nearest corner and waiting for people to show up. Instead, you must go out to certain places, engage in various activities, and begin to extend yourself in order for friendship to begin to take root in your life.

Neil came to our church as an assistant pastor, and Marcia and he were just a few years younger than Marcy and I. One day several months after his arrival, Neil called me up and said that his wife and he wanted to get together with us over coffee to get acquainted. I think this was the first time that someone we hardly knew had called us up to initiate a friendship.

We sat down in a local restaurant over coffee with Neil and Marcia and began to get to know them. They initiated most of the conversation, asking us about ourselves, our growing up years, our marriage. It was a wonderful time, and from this first meeting a lasting friendship grew. Neil and Marcia represent to me what it means to be proactive about friendship.

How can you begin to actively seek a friendship? First, you have to take a look at yourself to ascertain your strengths and limitations with regards to friendship. Then you should look at how to open up to other men to begin friendships. We will consider ways to perform this inventory and then to open up. Finally, we'll consider what is involved in maintaining friendships.

TAKING INVENTORY

What do you have to offer as a person? That bold question has a simple answer: what you have to offer is you. You don't need lots of money. You don't need exciting hobbies and pastimes. You just need to be a person who is willing to extend himself in friendship. That will be enough.

But let's consider again several elements in your personage that make it easier for you to reach out in friendship. Take the "Friendship Quiz" on page 201. You may want to take out a sheet of paper and write out each question, or you may simply put your answer after each question. The answer is a number from 1 to 10, with 1 representing "not at all" and 10 "almost always" (5 is "sometimes," 8 is "usually," for example). Afterward, if you have an accountability group or a good friend, you can show your list for verification.

THE FRIENDSHIP QUIZ
(Place a number from 1 to 10 in blank.)

1. Am I a caring person? The caring person is one who centers on other people. _____

2. Am I an honest person? To what extent am I "honest" with myself, my behavior conforming to what I say; and to what extent am I honest with others? _____

3. Can I keep another person's confidence? This creates safety for the other person. _____

4. Am I loyal to a friend, willing to stay with him during tough times? _____

5. Can I be myself around others? Am I comfortable with who I am and the person that God has made me to be? Or am I constantly molding myself to the expectations of others, hoping to gain approval from them? _____

6. Am I accountable? Can I point to a person in this world who truly knows me and who can point out my faults? _____

7. Am I available when people ask for help or my company? _____

8. Do I take full responsibility for what I say and do? _____

9. Is Jesus my friend, someone I tell about my hopes, fears, and needs on a regular basis? _____

Those questions that score below five are the areas where you will need to begin working.

Here are some guidelines and examples of each element in action, to help you to complete the friendship quiz.

1. Am I a caring person? The caring person is one who centers on other people. Not that he is always nurturing other people. Nurture is not a good strategy to be used indiscriminately with every need that appears. One of the greatest hindrances to friendship is people who focus primarily on themselves, their interests, their needs, their activities. Conversations have a way of revolving around what they've been doing lately.

Mark was the consummate caring person. Whenever there was a crisis, he would be there. He lent people his things—tools, cars, clothes, whatever—without a question. He was a great listener, attempting to see the other person's point of view without interjecting his own opinions. He would never think of 'grandstanding' at social functions by grabbing the attention to himself. He'd usually seek out the person who seemed to be hanging back disconnected from everyone else at the party. And as you can probably guess, Mark had many friends.

2. Am I an honest person? Earlier in the book we spoke of honesty. Honesty really goes in two directions—to myself and to others. Honesty with self means what I say matches the way I act toward people (or congruence). When word and deed don't match, I am not being honest with myself. I may think, for example, that I am a caring person, but people perceive me as indifferent and even aloof in my dealings with them.

The second part of honesty has to do with whether I am honest with other people. I may be honest within myself, but I have a tendency to not be truthful with others with whom I deal. As a result, people will begin to hold me at a distance, not finding me a trustworthy person.

3. Can I keep another person's confidence? It's so refreshing to have people who are safe, people with whom you can share your darkest secrets, knowing full well that those secrets are safe and will go no further. Such people have many friends as well as deep friendships, because depth comes as two people are willing to open more and more of their lives to each other. To open more, though, risks more. As each becomes more vulnerable to rejection or betrayal of confidence, a safe person is crucial.

Carl was the kind of person whom others readily turned to for help. They knew that they could tell Carl anything, and it would stop with him. He was nonjudgmental when told of problems, though he could also confront when people strayed out of line. But more than anything else, he kept his mouth shut with information given to him.

4. *Am I loyal?* Can you stick by a friend in the midst of crisis and difficulty? Or has your tendency been to move away when things got rough? When people begin to speak against your friend, have you stuck up for him, or have you kept silent or even joined in ridiculing your friend?

Ray had been a good friend to Bob for years. They had both become very successful in business, had joined the same country club and church, lived in the same upscale neighborhood, and generally spent a great deal of time together. Most of their other friends came from the club and church also.

Then Bob suffered a terrible financial reversal. He went bankrupt and lost practically everything he had. Along with his money, Bob lost nearly all his friends—except Ray. Ray stuck by Bob, even though an enormous gap had now opened between them in terms of their standards of living. Bob was embarrassed with his situation and embarrassed when Ray came around to his modest home, now far from the neighborhood where they both had lived. But Ray kept telling him, "Bob, we're friends through thick and thin. I guess this is thin, but I'll be there for you." Ray knows the meaning of loyalty.

5. *Can I be myself around others?* Do I experience freedom in my life? Am I comfortable with who I am and the person God has made me to be? Or am I constantly molding myself to the expectations of others, hoping to gain approval from them? Can I disagree with people? A person free to be himself also is comfortable letting his friends have other friends.

Rick is a man who is confident in himself. He knows what he believes. He has a set of core values from which he will not deviate. If you met him, you would say that he is quietly comfortable with himself. In conversation, he will disagree if he objects to what the speaker is saying. But people rarely find him objectionable. He is supremely respectful of people generally, even when he is at odds with them. He's even free to change his mind from time to time and admit that he was wrong.

6. *Am I accountable?* Men in particular do not like people looking over their shoulders, giving suggestions, correcting their

work. Can I point to a person in this world who truly knows me, and who can point out my faults?

Phil had struggled with pornography since he was a young adolescent. At certain times he would be overwhelmed with the desire to purchase magazines or go downtown to see live shows of naked women. But Phil was also a friend of Jesus, and he knew this was displeasing to Him. So he joined a small group of men that got together regularly to pray and read the Bible and hold each other accountable. Phil was honest about his struggles with pornography. To his amazement, two other men in the group of five also admitted their own struggles with it. Together, each week these men would be honest and hold each other accountable, and the struggles for Phil were greatly diminished.

7. *Am I available to help*? Can people count on me? Or am I always too busy to get involved when people call? It would be a good idea for the next couple of weeks to keep an hourly schedule of your day. This will help you get a good idea of what you are doing with your time. It may be most helpful if you would be willing to sit down with someone you respect and go over your schedule. Add up blocks of time (for example, work, golf, TV, time with wife) to see where you are spending the greatest part of your week. To be a friend, you must have time when you are available to your friends.

Mel was a man who was very regimented. He was always where he was supposed to be, and doing what he was supposed to do. Mel saw the importance of friendships in his life, so he regularly scheduled times to be with his friends. He also was willing at a moment's notice to drop everything if a friend in crisis called.

8. *Do I take full responsibility for what I say and do*? Or do I tend to blame other people and situations for all that is wrong with me?

Roy was one of those fellows who never could take responsibility for his own actions. Whenever something went wrong, someone else was to blame. He pushed off responsibility onto his wife, his work associates, the government, or God. He was always in a victim position. As a result, people found it difficult and annoying to be with Roy, and he had few friends.

9. *Is Jesus my friend*? To have the author of all relationships as a personal friend is truly an honor. And yet he has invited us to do that very thing.

Matt felt as though he needed few other people in his life. He was powerful and somewhat famous in his town where he had sat on the city council and run two successful businesses. Then the bottom seemed to fall out of his life. His wife threatened to leave him. He couldn't get reelected to the council. A new highway took business away. He began to drink heavily.

At this low point in his life, Matt turned to Christ. His life was transformed. He had never experienced a friendship like this before. Added to the impact was the community of friendships he found in his new church. Now he was surrounded by people who cared. Matt found that knowing Christ as a friend can make everything new.

AVAILABLE FOR FRIENDSHIPS

Getting Started

If you have few friends, you may not know how to get started. "Should I put an ad in the paper?" That's not necessary. The following suggestions all involve one thing: making your life an inviting life, one that draws people to you. Remember, too, to start slow. You can't make a flower grow by pulling at it.

Being Available

I've made this point over and over in this book, but it's important enough to repeat one more time. If you want to make friends, you have to find time in your schedule to be available. This is going to require consciously and proactively marking out specific times. For many of you this will be extremely painful, but it must be done. If you have trouble setting aside time, you may need to go to an older, experienced man whom you respect (possibly a former mentor) who can sit down with you and go over your priorities and help you eliminate extraneous entries in your weekly calendar.

Making Small Talk

My friend Tom Eisenman wrote a helpful book called *Everyday Evangelism* that considers all the common, everyday occurrences where it is possible to hook up with people with a view toward friendship and evangelism. One of the most helpful ideas Tom suggests concerns small talk.[1] Yet time and again I have found men who are extremely uncomfortable with small talk.

Many men who have found great success and reknown as public speakers and preachers have been afflicted with an inability to carry on small talk. I wondered about this inability. The trouble with small talk is that it is unstructured (unlike a prepared speech), and usually nothing truly meaningful by way of skills or knowledge is ever imparted. It's merely a way of being with people. But it's a very important part of being with people. It's the bridge to more meaningful conversations and to deeper relationships. The linguist Deborah Tannen says it best. "Small talk is crucial to maintain a sense of camaraderie when there is nothing special to say."[2] Small talk keeps us connected.

In his book, Eisenman mentions topics that are perfect for small talk: hobbies, current events, sports, places people have gone, etc. I personally like to think of things that are important to people, and make small talk about that. So I focus on the person I'm talking to. People who are not good at small talk tend to either avoid it altogether, or they take it as an occasion to talk about themselves. But people don't want to talk about you. They want to talk about themselves. So small talk centers on what is important to them.

I then have a pocketful of questions that I can ask to engage that person in small talk. If you center on the interests of the other person, you'll have no trouble and be on your way. Probably the best place to start is with a man's work. "What interesting projects are you working on now?" I enjoy having men tell me about what they do. Even if I'm fairly well acquainted with a particular occupation, I have found that everyone experiences his work differently. So I'm interested in what interests him about his job. I'll also ask, "What first got you interested in doing this?"

Writing Notes

Recently I read in our newspaper that a man attending our church had just passed the state bar exam. I really don't know him very well, but I know this is a great occasion for him; I keep a stack of notecards in my desk for just such occasions. I took one out, looked up his name in the church directory, and jotted him a note of congratulations.

Through the years I've learned that people love to receive little thoughtful notes at special times in their lives. A friend of mine gave me the idea to have some four by six note cards made up with my name printed at the top and matching envelopes. This has made it much easier for me to jot notes to people. I then bought a roll of stamps to accompany the pile of cards, and I was ready to go. I use these a lot with my friends, now scattered across the world, to keep up and let them know I'm thinking of them. I also use these with people I don't know very well, but who I know would appreciate a communication.

Serving People Practically

Eisenman once wrote about the power of people serving others. A woman he knew spent her childhood in a neighborhood where several Christian families lived. These families were truly spiritual light in the middle of that neighborhood. Whenever it snowed, people would wake up to find their walks and driveways already shoveled. When folks went away on vacation, lawns were mowed, gardens tended, papers picked up. These Christian families went out of their way to find small ways in which they could serve.[3]

Look around your office, your neighborhood, your church, or your club. Begin to notice small ways in which you can be of service to people. If you're the boss, this will be even more powerful to your employees as they see you serving them.

The servant posture automatically draws people to you. They begin to see in your life a quality that is very enticing. As you more frequently assume a servant's mentality, opportunities will begin to present themselves to you: the work day at the church, the man across the way who needs his coffee cup filled, the neighbor who's caring for sick parents across town who needs small favors around the house.

Allowing People to Serve You

Do you realize that you serve other people when you allow them to serve you? It's true. But this is also extremely difficult for the average man to manage. Men like the high status positions where they can be the giver, not the receiver. People will seek to serve you in many different places at various times. Someone may want to pick up your check at a restaurant. Another may want to come by and mow your lawn when you're sick. Each of these people offers you a gift. To reach out and receive it graciously is to serve the giver of the gift.

Finding Variety in Life

"Get a life, Dad!" My kids like to say this to me. They tend to say it to me when I'm looking at a particular situation in a very narrow way. Many men, especially those who are in their late twenties and thirties and who are climbing career ladders, become one dimensional in their lives. They pour their energy into work. What is left over is doled out sparingly to their family. Hobbies are neglected. Sporting activities are left behind. Vacations are forsaken. And, of course, these men have few friends.

Have you always wanted to oil paint, but never found the time? Now is a good time to think of taking it up. Have you thought of joining a soccer team for adults your age? Consider joining it. Have you wanted to serve on a church board, but have always turned down the offers when presented? Think again. I'm not advocating crowding your life with so many activities that you are never home. That is very dangerous. But each of us needs to branch out into other dimensions and bring into play gifts God has granted us. When we do this, we will enjoy pursuits that distract us from the stresses of work as well as bring out sides to our personalities that often lie dormant.

This will require a hard look at your schedule. It will also require accountability to trusted men who can keep you from becoming unbalanced.

Being Generous

If you are a generous person, you are willing to share all of the benefits that you have received in this life. You are a person who first realizes that all you have comes from God. These are all gifts. And as a result you are extremely grateful. Remember, all that you have ultimately has been bestowed by God. Even if you worked hard for it, God was always there providing all of the conditions—past and present—that were critical for you to accomplish what you did.

Nothing draws people more quickly to a person than acts of giving. Nothing drives people away faster than a person who grasps tightly the things he has acquired. We were at a party once and playing volleyball in the backyard. The ball was inadvertently hit into an azalea bush. My friend Dan went to retrieve it, and the owner of the bush and host of the party became extremely agitated. He screamed at Dan to be careful and reprimanded him for not extracting the ball more gently. Needless to say, there were few other parties at this man's house.

My friend Tom is one of the most generous people I have known. He told me a number of years ago that he always buys whatever the kids at the front door at supper time are selling. Up until that time, I had always thought of these kids as irritations, coming at inconvenient hours to try to sell me things to raise money for their particular projects. Tom also went out of his way to give to people, even at the risk of being "used" by people. He seemed to think that if he was going to err, it would be on the side of generosity. Tom is a man blessed with many friends.

Being Hospitable

Robert Roberts has a nice, simple definition for hospitality. He says it's "welcoming into your home territory people who don't belong there,"and then sharing "the benefits of one's home territory" with those people.[4] It really doesn't take much territory to have some place to invite a guest for fellowship. It can even be the heating grate where the homeless man lives. Roberts goes on to distinguish generosity from hospitality, noting that the generous person gives of what he has received. The hospitable person includes fellowship along with his generosity. He not only shares what he has, he takes the person home to be with him.[5]

In the final analysis, Christians are people who are just passing through. All of our territory and possessions are temporary. In this sense, there really isn't as much difference between the homeless man living on a grate in the middle of town, or the multimillionaire living in an exclusive penthouse near Central Park in Manhattan. But no matter where I happen to live, I do stake out my territory and my possessions, and as I open these up to people, I become a man of hospitality.

SMALL STEPS TO BEGIN

Now it's time to reach out into the community and make contact. Here are four simple steps to initiate the friendship:

1. Think of one or two men who would make possible candidates as friends. Think of people to whom you feel a natural affinity. Start your search at work, church, at your

club. Narrow your candidates down to just one. Begin to pray for him.

2. Ask that one person to breakfast or lunch. Tell him you have no agenda, you just want to get to know him better.

3. Be as clear as possible about your expectations. Tell this person that you are interested in deepening relationships in your life. Realize that the other person may not at this point want a friendship with you. If he says this, implicitly or explicitly, thank him for his candor. There may be a time in the future when the two of you can make contact. If he is interested, set a regular time for the next two months. I wouldn't set an open-ended agreement for the two of you to get together. You need a short trial period to see if being together is a good and helpful thing.

4. Set some sort of agenda. Although being with each other should be enough, men typically are nervous at first with no agenda. Pick a book or a passage of Scripture that you want to go over together.

If you are a younger man, it would be a good idea to begin seeking a mentor. This could be one of several people: a respected man in your career field to help mentor you in your vocation; a respected older man who has walked with Christ for a long time to mentor you spiritually; or an older man who can just be your friend. Pray that God will put the right man/men in your path. Then, as God leads, begin to ask men to mentor you.

If you are an older man, consider being a mentor to a young man. Pray that God would put before you a candidate or two who could benefit from your expertise.

HOW TO KEEP FRIENDSHIPS

Once a friendship begins to develop, it would seem easy to maintain. But like any important commitment, it requires work on your part. Here are several ways to help the friendship continue and flourish.

Stay in touch. Nothing kills friendship quicker than a lack of communication. I now have friends in almost every part of the world. To keep these friendships, I realize that I have to maintain communication. For some this has merely been a note or a call once a year. For one friend, I've made a cassette tape periodically to make sure that he knows all that I'm doing. He'll then return the cassette to me with his own stories. If you make friendship a priority, you'll need to stay in touch with your friends.

Do things together. Finding time to be with each other is essential. It is also important that both partners in the friendship initiate activities periodically (remember the need for reciprocity in friendship). Friendships grow particularly strong when friends find time to do things together.

Do things for each other. Remember the part about being a servant. There will be numerous opportunities when you will be able to serve your friend or allow your friend to serve you. The more you find and exploit these opportunities to serve, the deeper your friendship will become.

Continue to open your lives to each other. Friendship will bring about closeness. The sense of closeness will deepen as you and your friend are able to be more open with each other. Express to one another your goals and dreams, your struggles, your questions and doubts about life.

FORMALIZING THE RELATIONSHIP

Should we be formal about this? Now that you have a friend about whom you care deeply, you may want to begin to discuss with him the nature of how deep the relationship truly is. This could be dangerous. Your friend may not feel the relationship is as important to him as it feels to you. That's all right; it happens all the time.

But as the two of you find that your friendship is deepening, you may want to begin to articulate the nature of the relationship more. Covenants make for safe places, so you may also want to make some sort of covenant with each other. This could be a simple little ceremony where the two of you vow to stay in touch, to keep each other accountable, to pray for each other daily, and to be with each other as schedules permit.

Hopefully, in reading this book, you have come to appreciate the importance of friendship for your own life. It protects and strengthens our lives like bonds of iron. The joys of someone who knows you, cares, and accepts you are found in testimonies of many men who, like a U.S. Senate chaplain and a world-traveling consultant (chapter 7), find a true friend.

The material in the chapters and "Take Action" are practical and should be sufficient for you to begin your journey (or continue it) in friendships. I urge you not to delay that journey. Begin today to pray for men to enter your life and form friendships with you that will be life-changing. Then take that all important step of reaching out to men, initiating the contact, so that friendship can begin in your life.

TAKE ACTION

1. Small talk is an art few men learn or are comfortable with. The best small talkers are those people who can ask the best questions. If you aren't good at small talk, sit down before you go to you next party and make a list of generic questions that you can use with people. Here's a partial list:

   "What plans do you have for the summer?"

   "Tell me what you're reading these days."

   "What's the most fascinating project you have going at work?"

   "When you're not at work, how do you like to spend your time?"

   "If you could retire tomorrow, what would you do?"

   Now think of at least two more questions you can ask at a gathering and list them below:

   _____

   _____

2. Review five of the suggestions for getting started in a friendship: being available, writing notes, serving people, finding diversity in life, and being hospitable. During the next four weeks look for opportunities to practice two of these suggestions. Then just do it.

NOTES

Chapter 1: Do You Fear Friendships?

1. Jerry White, "A Friend on All Accounts," *Moody*, July/August 1991, 50–54; and Fred Hignell III, "Sharing the Paddle," *Moody*, July/August 1991, 51–54.

2. White, "A Friend," 54.

3. Ibid.

4. George Barna, *What Americans Believe* (Ventura, Calif.: Regal, 1991), 74.

5. David Smith, *The Friendless American Male* (Ventura, Calif.: Regal, 1983), 15.

6. Bert Decker, *You've Got to be Believed to be Heard* (New York: St.Martin's, 1991), 48ff.

7. Ibid., 47.

8. C. S. Lewis, *The Four Loves* (New York: Harcourt Brace Jovanovich, 1960), 91.

Chapter 3: How Did We Get This Way?

1. Robert A. Caro, *The Years of Lyndon Johnson. The Path to Power* (New York: Knopf, 1982), 330–31.

2. Lyman Coleman. Story told at Community Presbyterian Church, Danville, California, October 1990.

3. Ralph Keyes, "If Only I Could Say, 'I Love You.'" *Parade*, February 7, 1993, 4.

4. Eric McCollum, "Between Fathers and Sons," *Family Therapy Networker* 12, no. 3:40–46.

5. Stephen Covey, *The Seven Habits of Highly Effective People* (New York: Simon & Schuster, 1989), 18–19.

6. John Gray, *Men Are from Mars, Women Are from Venus* (New York: Harper Collins, 1992), 17.

7. Ibid., 67–70.

8. Walter Trobisch, *The Misunderstood Man* (Downers Grove, Ill.: InterVarsity, 1983), 35.

9. Letty C. Pogrebin, *Among Friends* (New York: McGraw-Hill, 1987), 253–78.

Chapter 4: How Friendships Work

1. Lewis Smedes, *Mere Morality* (Grand Rapids: Eerdmans, 1983), 160–61.

2. This account is an adaptation of the friendship of power of two Texas politicians, Sam Rayburn and Lyndon Johnson, and is based on their true story. For more information on their distinctive relationship, see Robert Caro, *The Years of Lyndon Johnson* (New York: Random House, 1983).

3. Malcolm Smith, "Loyalty: The Key to Kingdom Living." Tape #1. Malcolm Smith Ministry; P.O. Box 29747, San Antonio, TX 78229.

4. Joel D. Block, *Friendship* (New York: Collier, 1980), 55.

5. David Augsburger, *Caring Enough to Confront* (Ventura, Calif.: Regal, 1973), 20.

6. Robert N. Bellah, et al., *Habits of the Heart* (New York: Harper & Row, 1985), 115.

7. "Take Action" activities 2 and 3 are adapted from James Osterhaus, *Building Strong Male Relationships* (Chicago: Moody, 1993), 28–29.

Chapter 5: Are You Ready for Friendships?

1. The elements of love in the section "Ready for Love" are a summary of the ideas found throughout Smedes' book *Love Within Limits* (Grand Rapids: Eerdmans, 1978).

2. Stephen R. Covey, *The Seven Habits of Highly Effective People* (New York: Simon & Schuster, 1989), 72-73.

3. Ibid., 92.

4. Murray Bowen, *Family Therapy in Clinical Practice* (New York: Aronson, 1978), 472–75.

Chapter 6: Friendship and Communication

1. Bert Decker, *You've Got To Be Believed To Be Heard* (New York: St. Martin's, 1992), 81–116.

2. Ibid., 117–52.

3. James Patterson and Peter Kim, *The Day America Told the Truth* (New York: Prentice-Hall, 1991), 45.

4. Deborah Tannen, *You Just Don't Understand* (New York: Ballantine, 1990), 24–25.

5. John Gray, *Men Are from Mars, Women Are from Venus* (New York: Harper Collins, 1992), 16.

6. Ibid., 17–24.

7. Tannen, *Understand*, 123–48.

Chapter 8: Friendships During the Early Seasons of Life

1. Daniel Levinson, *The Seasons of a Man's Life* (New York: Ballantine, 1978).

2. Verne Becker, *The Real Man Inside* (Grand Rapids: Zondervan, 1992), 61.

3. James Patterson and Peter Kim, *The Day America Told the Truth* (New York: Prentice-Hall, 1991), 6.

4. Robert Bly, *Iron John* (Reading, Pa.: Addison-Wesley, 1990), 15.

5. D. J. Levinson, C. M. Darrow, D. B. Klein, M. H. Levinson, & B. McKee, "Periods in the Adult Development of Men: Ages 18 to 45." *The Counseling Psychologist* 6 (1976):23.

6. Ford's mentoring program is called Arrow Leadership. For more information, write Leighton Ford Ministries; 6230 Fairview Rd, Suite 300; Charlotte, NC 28210.

7. Levinson, *Seasons*, 140.

8. Ibid., 139.

9. Jim Conway, *Men in Midlife Crisis* (Elgin, Ill.: David C. Cook, 1978), 12.

10. Levinson, *Seasons*, 192.

11. Ibid., 199.

12. Conway, *Midlife*, 281.

Chapter 9: Friendships During the Later Years

1. Letty C. Pogrebin, *Among Friends* (New York: McGraw-Hill, 1987), 360.

Chapter 10: Spirituality: Friendship with God and with People

1. James Houston, *The Transforming Friendship* (London: Lion, 1988), 11.

2. Richard Lovelace, *Renewal as a Way of Life* (Downers Grove, Ill.: Inter-Varsity, 1985), 37.

3. Lawrence Richards, *A Practical Theology of Spirituality* (Grand Rapids: Zondervan, 1987), 21.

4. Ibid., 50.

5. James Houston, "Devotional Aspects of Discipleship." Lecture presented to C. S. Lewis Institute, 29 May 1984.

6. Richards, *Spirituality*, 67. Richards calls the seven characteristics "aspects of human life." The seven are: identity, intimacy, sinfulness, lordship, mortality, holiness, and commitment. My discussion is based largely on those seven aspects, which Richards discussed from pages 66 to the end of the book. I highly recommend *A Practical Theology of Spirituality* for your reading.

7. Ibid., 66.

8. Ibid., 97.

9. Houston, *Transforming*, 33.

10. Richards, *Spirituality*, 102.

11. Richard Foster, *Celebration of Discipline* (New York: Harper & Row, 1978), 30–40.

12. Ibid., 30.

13. Richards, *Spirituality*, 140.

14. Ibid., 143.

15. Ibid., 144.

16. David Augsburger, *Caring Enough to Confront* (Ventura, Calif.: Regal, 1973), 12–14.

17. Ibid., 15.

Chapter 11: Authority, Integrity, and Other Marks of a Spiritual Relationship

1. Lawrence Richards, *Expository Dictionary of Biblical Words* (Grand Rapids: Zondervan, 1985), 417–18.

2. Richards, *Spirituality*, 151.

3. Ibid., 159.

4. Richards, *Spirituality*, 166.

5. Ibid., 181.

6. Ibid., 186.

7. Richards, *Expository*, 339.

8. Richards, *Spirituality*, 198–200.

9. Lewis Smedes, *Mere Morality* (Grand Rapids: Eerdmans, 1983), 24.

10. Richards, Spirituality, 65.

11. Ibid., 238.

12. Foster, *Celebration*, 117–22.

Chapter 12: Wives and Other Women as Friends

1. Harville Hendrix, *Getting the Love You Want* (New York: Harper & Row, 1988), 8-14.

2. Ibid., 88-92.

3. Tom Skinner, address to Truro Church, Fairfax, Virginia, on 31 December 1984.

4. Ellyn Bader and Peter Pearson, *In Quest of the Mythical Mate* (New York: Brunner/Mazel, 1988), 3.

5. Ibid., 2.

6. Lillian Rubin, *Just Friends* (New York: Harper & Row, 1985), 158–60.

7. Rubin, 158.

8. Tom Eisenman, *Temptations Men Face* (Downers Grove, Ill.: InterVarsity, 1990), 89-93.

9. The actual steps to an affair, as outlined by Eisenman, are readiness, alertness, innocent meeting, intentional meeting, public lingering, private lingering, purposeful isolating, and pleasureable isolating. At this point touch enters; the final four steps are affectionate embracing, passionate embracing, capitulation, and acceptance.

10. Lewis Smedes, *Mere Morality* (Grand Rapids: Eerdmans, 1983), 170.

11. Ibid., 171.

12. Letty Pogrebin, *Among Friends* (New York: McGraw-Hill, 1987), 337.

Chapter 13: When a Friendship Fades

1. Argyle and A. Furnham, "Sources of Satisfaction and Conflict in Long-term Relationships," *Journal of Marriage and the Family*, August 1983.

2. Letty Pogrebin, *Among Friends* (New York: McGraw-Hill, 1987), 67.

3. Lewis Smedes, *Forgive and Forget* (New York: Pocket Books, 1984), 31–37; these two reasons for failed relationships are also mentioned in Pogrebin, *Among Friends*, 67.

4. Ibid., 33–34.

Chapter 14: How to Begin

1. Tom Eisenman, *Everyday Evangelism* (Downers Grove, Ill.: InterVarsity, 1987), 34–37.

2. Deborah Tannen, *You Just Don't Understand* (New York: Ballantine, 1990), 102.

3. Eisenman, *Everyday*, 37.

4. Robert Roberts, *Taking the Word to Heart* (Grand Rapids: Eerdmans, 1993), 242–43.

5. Ibid., 243.